WITHDRAWN

THE DIGITAL WORLD

DIGITAL SECURITY
CYBER TERROR AND CYBER SECURITY

001000010110
011000011100
110110001011
011011011010
100110010100
100011000011
001000010110
011000011100
110110001011
011011011010
100110010100
100011000011
001000010110
011000011100

THE DIGITAL WORLD

DIGITAL COMMUNICATIONS

DIGITAL GAMES

DIGITAL MUSIC

DIGITAL RESEARCH

DIGITAL SECURITY

DIGITAL VIDEO

THE DIGITAL WORLD

DIGITAL SECURITY
CYBER TERROR AND CYBER SECURITY

001000010110
011000011100
110110001011
011011011010
100110010100
100011000011
001000010110
011000011100
110110001011
011011011010
100110010100
100011000011
001000010110
011000011100
110110001011

ANANDA MITRA, PH.D.

CHELSEA HOUSE
PUBLISHERS
An imprint of Infobase Publishing

PORTER MEMORIAL BRANCH LIBRARY
NEWTON COUNTY LIBRARY SYSTEM
6191 HIGHWAY 212
COVINGTON, GA 30016

Digital Security: Cyber Terror and Cyber Security

Copyright © 2010 by Infobase Publishing

All rights reserved. No part of this book may be reproduced or utilized in any form or by any means, electronic or mechanical, including photocopying, recording, or by any information storage or retrieval systems, without permission in writing from the publisher. For information, contact:

Chelsea House
An imprint of Infobase Publishing
132 West 31st Street
New York NY 10001

Library of Congress Cataloging-in-Publication Data
Mitra, Ananda, 1960–
  Digital security : cyber terror and cyber security / Ananda Mitra.
    p. cm. — (The digital world)
  Includes bibliographical references and index.
  ISBN 978-0-8160-6791-6 (hardcover)
  1. Computer crimes—Juvenile literature. 2. Cyberterrorism—Prevention—Juvenile literature.
3. Internet—Security measures—Juvenile literature. 4. Computer networks—Security
measures—Juvenile literature. 5. Computer security—Juvenile literature. I. Title. II. Series.

  HV6773.M58 2010
  364.16'8—dc22

                                                                    2009052512

Chelsea House books are available at special discounts when purchased in bulk quantities for businesses, associations, institutions, or sales promotions. Please call our Special Sales Department in New York at (212) 967-8800 or (800) 322-8755.

You can find Chelsea House on the World Wide Web at http://www.chelseahouse.com

Text design by Annie O'Donnell
Cover design by Takeshi Takahashi
Composition by Newgen Imaging Systems
Cover printed by Bang Printing, Brainerd, MN
Book printed and bound by Bang Printing, Brainerd, MN
Date printed: May 2010
Printed in the United States of America

10 9 8 7 6 5 4 3 2 1

This book is printed on acid-free paper.

All links and Web addresses were checked and verified to be correct at the time of publication. Because of the dynamic nature of the Web, some addresses and links may have changed since publication and may no longer be valid.

Contents

Preface

These days, it is not unusual for 10- to 12-year-olds to be publishing their own Web sites or for second and third graders to begin computer classes. At the same time, computer games are becoming increasingly popular as major publishing houses continue to churn out educational computer programs for children in preschool. At the other end of the spectrum, technological know-how has become a requirement for most jobs in an increasingly digital world, as the computer has become a common tool in most professions. Even the often-mentioned "digital divide" between those who have access to computers and those who do not is being bridged with the development of tools such as the XD computer designed by the Massachusetts Institute of Technology Media Laboratory and the availability of computers at libraries and schools. As people become more reliant on digital devices to perform everyday tasks, these modern conveniences become commonplace.

Even though there are many different kinds of computers available for everyday use—ranging from gadgets like the BlackBerry to specially made computers for playing computer games—all the machines operate on the fundamental system of ones and zeros called binary, invented in the seventeenth century. Although it might appear that computers and newly developed digital products are "new" technologies, the seeds of modern digital technologies were planted nearly three centuries ago and grew with the research of legendary scholars and engineers such as Gottfried Leibniz and others.

The relevance of digital technologies in everyday life often has been overshadowed by market-driven hype about new technologies that appear to be introduced at a breakneck speed, which leaves so many people scrambling to catch up to the latest gadget. This result, however, is the surface representation of deeper changes in society that are taking place with the adoption of digital tools in different aspects of everyday life. THE DIGITAL WORLD is a set of volumes that aims to explore the whole spectrum of applications, describing how digital systems influence society and helping readers understand the nature of digital systems and their many interacting parts. The set covers major applications of digital systems and includes the following titles:

- *Digital Communications*
- *Digital Games*
- *Digital Music*
- *Digital Research*
- *Digital Security*
- *Digital Video*

Each volume in the set explores a wide range of material, explains the basic concepts of these applications, and then discusses the implications they have on everyday life. Because the number of possible topics is practically limitless, we focus on a sample of the most interesting and useful applications and tools and explain the basic principles of technology. Readers are encouraged to continue exploring the digital world with the guidance of our Further Resources section featured in each volume. The goal of these books is to encourage the reader to see the relevance of digital systems in all aspects of life, at the present time as well as in the past and in the years to come.

Acknowledgments

I would like to thank a group of people who made this book possible. My thanks first goes to my family in America and India who provided support and balance to my writing life. Appreciation also goes to my friends in Winston-Salem and colleagues at Wake Forest University who provided the encouragement throughout the entire process of doing the six books in this series. Thanks also goes to Elizabeth Oakes for providing photographs that illustrate the different components of the digital world and to Jodie Rhodes, who helped me overcome more than one challenge. Finally, I thank the editors for their patience and encouragement to ensure we create a worthy product. General thanks goes to the publisher for giving me this opportunity.

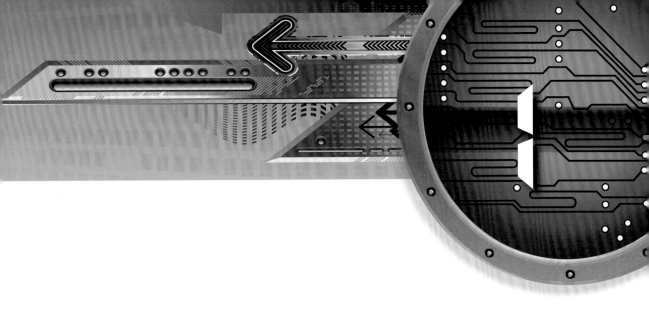

Digital Stalking

Everyone in the United States is issued a Social Security number that becomes a personal identity code used for many different transactions. When unscrupulous people gain access to this number, they can use it for fraudulent purposes. This happened to a family in Illinois, when the Social Security number of a seven-year-old child was stolen and used illegally in 2008. Gene Haschak of the *Daily Herald* reported that when the culprit was caught in Illinois, it was found that "he has used the Social Security card with the victim's information to obtain a truck, three separate jobs, gas and electrical service for his home, a credit card, unemployment benefits twice for a total of six months, and over $60,000 in pay and services." This illegal act of fraud, also known as identity theft, is not a new or an occasional incident; new technologies have simply opened up new threats and challenges to personal and public safety. New crimes are possible because a person's identity can be digitally produced, maintained, and manipulated. This chapter looks at the relationship between a person's actual self and his or her digital representation.

People and nations are concerned about their security and safety. They use soldiers to guard the borders between countries, police officers to offer protection inside the country, and locks on doors to keep intruders away from homes. The goal is to protect their space from enemies who might want to violate the space. The December 7, 1942, bombing of Pearl Harbor showed the American people that Japan was the enemy in World War II, just as the September 11, 2001, destruction of the World Trade Center in New York demonstrated that terrorists were bent on targeting Americans. Knowing one's enemy makes one stronger, since it is then possible to construct defenses against the possible enemy attacks. This is one of the reasons why nations require that everyone possess a legal passport before he or she is allowed into a country. The passport identifies a person, and a person who has been previously identified as a possible threat can be stopped from entering the country. This is just one of the ways in which national space is protected. Other ways range from satellite surveillance to border fences that help to protect geographic spaces.

The digital age poses a new vulnerability because digital spaces do not physically exist; cyberspace is built of binary data made up of numbers that reside on numerous computers across the world. A good way of thinking of cyberspace is to imagine it as a large number of computer files residing on millions of computers that are all connected by the Internet. Web sites are a part of this cyberspace, as are the countless e-mails sent daily by millions of people. Because cyberspace only exists virtually, it is impossible to touch it in the way one can touch a piece of rock. There are also no good ways to know who is in cyberspace, because anyone with access to a networked computer can access the Internet and cyberspace. In a world that has learned to protect its real spaces, border control officials often know who has entered a country or police can block off a space under attack by the enemy. It is far more difficult, however, to constantly trace who is in which part of cyberspace; there are too many people in cyberspace, and there are many good methods of hiding one's presence there.

Given these differences between physical space and cyberspace, the ways a person is vulnerable in cyberspace are harder to detect than the dangers in real space. The dangers in real space often have to do with physical injury, where someone can hit another person to break a bone. In cyberspace, there is no real tangible existence, but a person exists as a set of numbers, simply as information, which can become vulnerable because digital information can be easily transformed, stolen, and circulated throughout the Internet. In cyberspace, the attack could be on the information that represents someone, causing great personal, legal, or financial harm. Some individuals are at a greater risk than others because they have a larger presence in cyberspace.

DIGITALLY FINDING PEOPLE

It is now possible for most people all over the world to get on the Internet. In developed countries like the United States, a significant portion of people have Internet access in their homes from using their personal computers. Others have access to the Internet from places like schools, libraries, local universities, and other public institutions. There is access also through Internet cafés and other private institutions that are set up to allow people to connect to the Internet. According to the 2008 CIA World Factbook, there are an estimated 1.6 billion Internet users in the world, 231 million of whom reside in the United States. Internet availability is a little different in developing countries, but an increasing number of people are able to gain access.

In order to gain access to the Internet, an individual must have a computer connected to the Internet. User accounts can offer people access to different parts of the Internet; if one wants to subscribe to Internet-based information services that send periodic updates on topics like world news, the stock market, or the weather, then the user must establish an account with the service provider. Most of the time, the user provides information by completing a form that appears on the computer screen, and the information is stored in a computer information storage system called a database. The person disclosing the information usually does it in good faith, but that information can easily be compromised, as reported in an August 2006 article in *USA Today*. Reporters Michelle Kessler and Kevin Maney wrote how an employee of former Internet giant America Online (AOL), "without authorization, posted on the Internet the millions of search words typed in by 658,000 users over a three-month period." These words were typed in by users who never expected that the information would become publicly available, but one individual who had access to the information was able to violate the trust of the people who typed the words. While the search words might not be very critical to personal safety, people often give out other important information—such as date of birth, gender, Social Security number, or driver's license number—to specific Web sites in order to do a variety of activities, including online banking and social networking. This willingness to send such sensitive information out into cyberspace makes people vulnerable because such information can be misused similar to the search words.

In cyberspace, personal information is a representation of a real person. There are many ways of getting this information, including legally purchasing it. Often, when people disclose personal information to Web sites in exchange for a service or information, they have to accept a license agreement that can allow the company collecting the information to sell the identity information. Such sale of information happens routinely between large corporations, and people can be identified through that process. Information that is collected in a legitimate way, however, can also become compromised, and someone can easily access unprotected information. In May 2006, an employee of the U.S. Department of Veterans Affairs took home a computer with the personal records of 26 million American war veterans. When thieves stole this computer, the personal information of the millions of former soldiers became compromised.

There also are dishonest people who set up false Web sites that collect personal information. People visiting these Web sites could voluntarily give out information. This process is called phishing (pronounced "fishing"), since the process involves offering bait, in the form of a fake Web site, to a vulnerable user who will fall for the trick, eventually disclosing sensitive personal information. Phishing begins with sending out misleading e-mails requesting personal information, and people often misunderstand the purpose of the e-mail, or mistake it for a message from a legitimate business, accidentally disclosing this information to the criminals who originally sent the deceptive e-mail.

Finding information about people is usually accomplished by gaining the trust of the user. In most cases, this does not pose a problem for unscrupulous people, since the average user of the Internet has learned to trust legitimate Web sites to conduct online transactions. The phishing process and other Internet-based scams abuse this trust.

TRUST IN CYBERSPACE

In general, the term *cyberspace* describes the network of computers that are connected by the Internet. However, the word and the concept came into existence long before the Internet was invented. The word was first used by William Gibson, who described a fictional virtual space in his 1984 book, *The Neuromancer,* as cyberspace. In this book, the author describes a group of computer users who are able to enter a digital network, or cyberspace, by using any computer connected to the system. In real life, such a technology was being developed, where many computers, distant from one another, were connected using phone lines and satellite connections. When this was achieved, it was possible to create a new space that had no real existence but which people could enter to interact with others using a computer connected to the network. At that time, Gibson's term was used to describe the virtual space created by the network.

In the mid-1980s this network was restricted to some universities in Western Europe and North America and some government organizations in the same regions. It was mostly used by university professors and government employees to send electronic

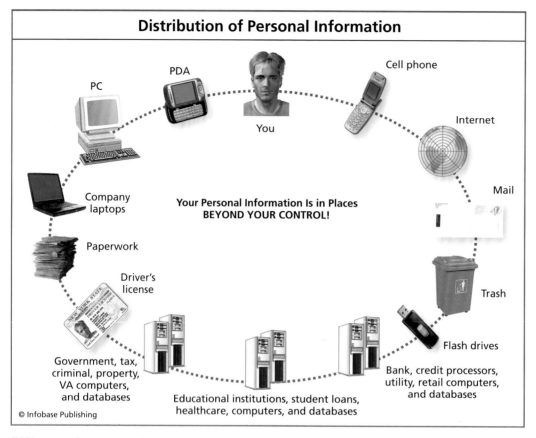

Distribution of Personal Information

PC

PDA

You

Cell phone

Internet

Mail

Company laptops

Your Personal Information Is in Places BEYOND YOUR CONTROL!

Paperwork

Driver's license

Trash

Flash drives

Government, tax, criminal, property, VA computers, and databases

Educational institutions, student loans, healthcare, computers, and databases

Bank, credit processors, utility, retail computers, and databases

© Infobase Publishing

Different elements of personal information are available in different kinds of gadgets and parts of the Internet. People store information on their computers, telephones, e-mail, and on paper. All of this information can become compromised, creating problems with privacy of information.

messages among the small number of users and for exchanging digital files among the users. The question of trust was unimportant because most of the users knew one another and they all needed to learn special skills in order to use the network.

Things changed when researchers were able to develop a simple computer program for average users to create texts that could be placed on one computer on the network, allowing anyone else with access to the network to read those text files. This language was invented by Tim Berners-Lee and was named hypertext markup language—often abbreviated as HTML. In addition, more computers began to connect to the network, which quickly grew into what we now know as the Internet, allowing anyone with access to log on and look up new information or meet other users. More people, who were not necessarily trained in computer programming, were able to get on the Internet through companies like America Online, or AOL, and Earthlink, both of which offered users e-mail addresses and accounts on the Internet.

As a result, more people began to obtain an identity on the Internet, and an increasing number of people could put up their own home pages on the Web. These pages could be read by anyone with access to the Internet and could display any information or message the author of the page wished to communicate to the world. The only way of knowing the author of a Web site is to read the material that is on the home page. Because many people tend to believe in whatever they read, trust in cyberspace is built by putting up truthful statements on the Web sites.

In real life, trust is often based on the type of interaction one has with an individual. In a school, for example, children often know which of their peers is likely to exaggerate, and thus those peers are not always to be trusted. In cyberspace, no such prior knowledge is available, and oftentimes, the only information is obtained by reading what a person says on his or her Web site or other documents the person puts up on the Internet. For this reason, trust and text are closely related in cyberspace, making it difficult to understand who can be trusted. Consequently, deception is easier in cyberspace.

DIGITAL DECEPTION

As mentioned, many people believe what they read, which opens up many opportunities for these people to be deceived. This process of deception has a history in other media like television, where video manipulation has existed for decades. That process has extended to the Web, as people often place false information on the Internet.

Dishonesty on the Internet can happen on any Web venue; chat rooms, forums, and even e-mail can include false information that is expressed in specific ways in order to get a reader to believe the message. Greek intellectuals like Aristotle have described how false logic and incorrect facts can be presented to deceive people. In such cases, the language of the text becomes particularly important, since skillful authors can easily convince the reader that what is being said is true. The reader would thus be deceived, eventually acting in a way that would be beneficial to the deceiver. For example, it is possible to create professional-looking Web sites that look like they represent nonprofit organizations asking for charitable donations. These Web sites are often so convincing that readers are tricked into donating money for what appears to be a good cause, but the money ends up profiting the deceiver. Several such Web sites were discovered after Hurricane Katrina devastated the Gulf Coast and the Louisiana city of New Orleans in 2005. Dishonest people put up Web sites asking for donations for the hurricane survivors, but the money just ended up going to the thieves who produced the Web sites.

Another way in which deception operates is by mimicking the signature styles of trustworthy authors. Deceivers can produce Web sites that look like the ones that are produced by well-known sources. A news organization like the BBC (British Broadcasting Company) has a Web site of its own; the news reported on that Web site is usually trustworthy and is based on real events that are happening around the world. Users of the Internet often recognize the specific text and visual style of such Web sites, and tend to trust sites that have this authoritative "look." Deceivers often take advantage of this trust by creating a Web site that looks similar to the work of the original author such as the BBC, and then spreading false information. This was the case in 2003, when a news site that looked like CNN.com made its appearance with completely false stories. Visitors to the site were fooled into believing the information was real because the visual presentation of the Web site appeared to be authentic. In fact, the site was so convincing that many other news reporters picked up the false stories from the Web site and reported them. Leander Kahney of *Wired* reported that "phony stories about the death of musician Dave Matthews, or the Olsen twins attending local universities, for example, appeared in a number of local newspapers, as well as regional radio and TV news reports." The other news organizations did not even bother to check the facts of the stories, since they appeared to come from a trusted source.

Another form of deception in cyberspace depends on false identities produced by dishonest users of the Internet. People who want to deceive offer false information about themselves, presenting a fake identity meant to fool people. Such identities are designed to generate trust that can then be abused. This could mean that a man can present himself as a woman, or an older person can claim to be someone much younger. Similarly, people can claim to live in a certain place when they live somewhere else.

Deception is done using both of these methods. Those who are focused on cheating people in cyberspace often use a combination of false information and false identity to gain the trust of unsuspecting users. As a result, the deceived user could disclose information that can be used to bring some form of harm to him or her.

MAKING REAL-LIFE CONNECTIONS USING CYBERSPACE

Cyberspace is built around connected computers that store large amounts of legitimate information, most of which is meant to benefit those seeking information. Increasingly, the Web is becoming a resource for finding information on just about anything one could be interested in. Users can take the most trustworthy information and make decisions based on what they have learned. Problems occur when decisions are based on incorrect information. For example, anyone can produce a convincing-looking weather prediction Web site, but if the prediction is false, then people relying on this untrustworthy Web site could be misinformed about the weather. It is the connection between the virtual information and real-life decisions that is important to consider when examining the way in which information can be abused.

The virtual world and the real world connect when virtual information about individuals is used to harm them in real life. There are many ways of doing this, and all follow the same principle: Find

ASSUMING NAMES IN CYBERSPACE

Users of the Internet usually have to obtain a username, a name that serves as a unique identifier for different Internet applications. No two users of the same Internet-based applications such as chat rooms, e-mails, and instant messaging software can have the same username. Users also have a password that protects them from someone misusing their account. There often is a large degree of freedom in choosing a username; since people often have similar or the same names in real life, users can be creative in adjusting their real name or coming up with something completely different, so that everyone who is called "John" can be on the Internet with his unique username.

In many Internet-based applications, the user must have a username to start the program, but he or she can also select another name to publicly represent him or her. There need not be any relationship between the real person and the name the person uses to identify himself or herself. For example, a man called Richard can take the name of a woman and call himself Linda in a chat room, and the other users would have little way of knowing that a deceptive identity was being used. In fact, users can create usernames that do not resemble common names. Usernames can include numbers and indicate interests or preference, creating more anonymity. Unlike other forms of communication where some nonverbal cues such as visual images, voice, and accent can offer some clues about the gender, age, and ethnicity of a person, in cyberspace, it is the name that has to be the source of all this information.

(opposite) Criminals who steal personal information often use it for financial purposes and create false credit card accounts and bank accounts to siphon money from the victim. Personal information can also be used to create other accounts that take advantage of the information obtained from the victim.

information about a person from the Internet and use it to change the real life of the person. For example, financial fraud is a common crime that uses financial information, like credit card numbers, to

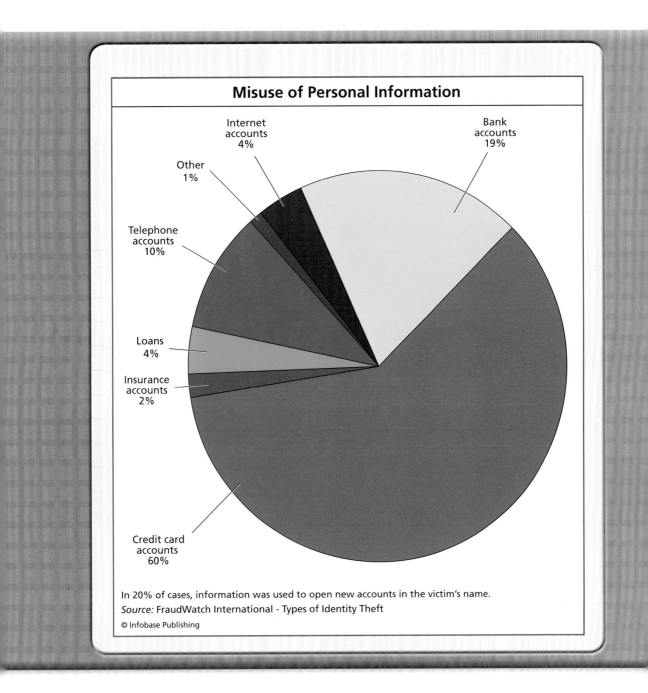

Misuse of Personal Information

Internet accounts 4%

Bank accounts 19%

Other 1%

Telephone accounts 10%

Loans 4%

Insurance accounts 2%

Credit card accounts 60%

In 20% of cases, information was used to open new accounts in the victim's name.

Source: FraudWatch International - Types of Identity Theft

© Infobase Publishing

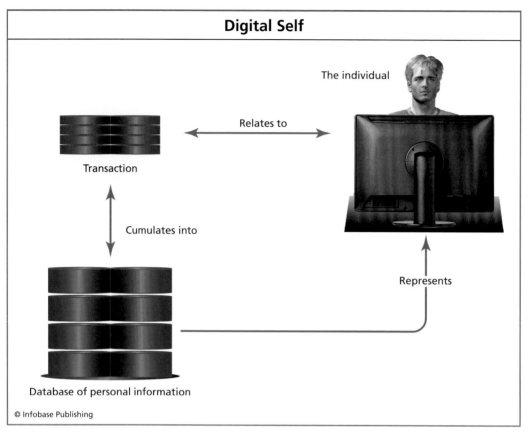

Digital Self

The individual

Relates to

Transaction

Cumulates into

Represents

Database of personal information

© Infobase Publishing

Whenever a person performs a digital transaction, it relates to a real human being who might have bought a product at a store using a credit card. The digital information is added to a large database of information that produces the digital self on the Internet that becomes a cumulation, or combination, of all the digital information.

steal money from unsuspecting victims. One of the largest such information breaches occurred in 2005, when 40 million Visa and MasterCard credit card numbers became available to criminals. As Jonathan Krim and Michael Barbaro of *The Washington Post* reported, "MasterCard is certain only that 68,000 of its numbers were taken by the hacker over an unknown amount of time before the breach was discovered. But because the hacker had access to the full database, it is difficult to say how many more numbers may have been taken." This kind of crime has become popular because large amounts of personal information are now digitally stored, and if that information falls into the wrong hands, it can be misused.

Digital information about an individual can also be used to cause physical or emotional harm. In this case, criminals would find information about a person from the Internet and then meet the individual face to face. These meetings could take place between people of different ages, where the meeting might be considered inappropriate, illegal, and perhaps even dangerous. For example, in a 2004 study based on data collected from a sample of law enforcement personnel in the United States, Janis Wolak, David Finkelhor, and Kimberly Mitchell of the University of New Hampshire reported in the *Journal of Adolescent Health* that "parents and professionals working with children need to discuss the reality and inadvisability of these relationships." The researchers are referring to relationships that begin on the Internet and then transform into real-life encounters between children 13 to 17 years old and adults who are older than 25.

Some people may think that the faceless, anonymous nature of cyberspace makes it a safe place. However, it is possible—in some cases, even easy—to make connections between digital information about a person and the real person because there are many ways in which the actual location of a person can be obtained from the digital information.

FINDING PEOPLE IN REAL LIFE USING THE COMPUTER

When looking for someone in real life, it is necessary to know the places the person inhabits, like the home one lives in, the school that one goes to, or the place where one works. It is possible to find the real person if one or more of those locations is known. One of the simplest ways to find someone's location is to ask him or her—and many Web sites do just that. For example, shopping sites ask for a physical address in order to ship their products to their online customers. In such situations, people readily disclose their real-life location, which could later become compromised and fall into criminal hands. There is little protection against such situations other than being aware that any information submitted to a Web site or discussed while on the Internet could fall into the wrong hands. With the increasing dependence on the Internet for many everyday activities, one can only hope that the information is adequately protected.

There are also indirect ways of gathering information without asking the person for personal information. Many popular Internet search programs can provide very specific location information about people that helps users find an address on a detailed map or even obtain satellite pictures of the place. Google, the most popular search tool on the Internet, offers the capability of searching for a person's address and phone number just by using the first and last name of a person and some general information about the location (such as the city where the person might live). This is possible because numerous companies maintain databases that store information about an individual. For example, many counties in the United States have satellite images of the area, the phone company has a list of phone numbers of its subscribers, the post office has a list of addresses, and all of these databases can be merged to produce an information database on an entire population of people, including all their personal details. It is then possible to search through this database to find information about a person. For example, there is a Web site called Reverse Phone Directory (http://www.reversephonedirectory.com) that can look up the name and address of a person based on a phone number.

People can also be located by tracing the computers that they use to connect to the Internet, because whenever a computer is connected, it is given a unique identifying number called the Internet Protocol number (IP number). For example, if a computer has the IP number 192.168.1.103, the last three digits identify the specific computer on the local network of computers in a person's home, and the other numbers indicate the kind of network a computer is on, as well as where the network is physically located. There are several tools available on the Internet that can identify a computer based on the

IP number. For example, a company called Whois.net advertises one of its services as such: "Use Whois By IP to figure out who owns an IP address or the location of where it is." These tools, when used by experts, can offer very specific information about the exact location of the computer. The user does not disclose any personal information, but the user can be located simply by finding the computer.

PROTECTING YOURSELF IN CYBERSPACE

With all the dangers that exist on the Internet, users must be proactive in protecting themselves from those who wish to use cyberspace to commit crimes. While many people simply decline to send their personal information to Web sites, this is unavoidable if a person wants to use any interactive online service. Online shopping, Internet banking, and even Facebook require a user to provide a certain amount of private information, rarely with the intention of sharing this information, which can potentially be exploited in illegal ways.

In order to keep their users' information secure, many Web sites, especially banks and credit card sites, will use several different methods to deter criminals from hacking into accounts. Users are often required to create complex passwords, featuring both letters and numbers, but these Web sites will also encrypt this information, or turn it into a secret code, after the user hits the "send" button. This information is later decoded when it is needed or being used. Other similar methods used by companies include investigating Web sites designed to resemble their own to trick users into providing usernames and passwords; instituting additional security measures like a security key that forces users to use their mouse to input information instead of the keyboard, which can be monitored by hackers; and session time outs, which log users out of their accounts after a certain amount of time to prevent others from seeing the personal information or using the account.

Many people who use the Internet for shopping, banking, and communication try to be vigilant, or fiercely aware, of the state of their information. Internet users will often pay credit bureaus to run credit checks on themselves to ensure that no one has been able to open up credit cards or bank accounts under their identities. While credit checks do not prevent identity theft or deter criminals from stealing your private information for their own use, they help make people aware of how they are exposing their personal information to the public and how easily someone else can use the information to their own advantage.

The digital world has changed our collective sense of security by making information vulnerable. New technologies have also offered an inexpensive and global communication system to allow illegitimate people and groups to develop an Internet presence. This process is particularly alarming with groups that spread hate.

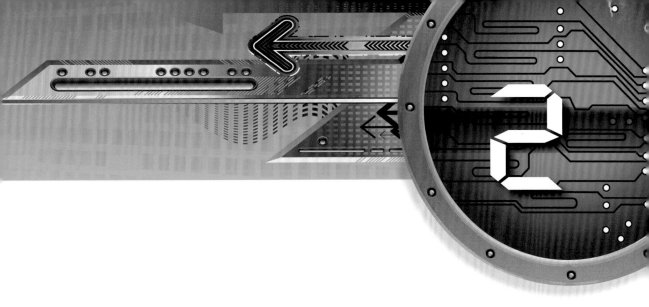

Digital Hate

Following the fall of the Taliban, a fundamentalist Muslim regime in Afghanistan, in the early 2000s, the extremist group al Qaeda moved many of its activities to the Internet. After the capture of the key Web promoter for al Qaeda in 2007, *The Economist* reported that "the Internet gives jihadists an ideal vehicle for propaganda, providing access to large audiences free of government censorship." These groups usually have a manifesto that ostracizes those outside the group, and they are able to use digital tools to spread their message of hate and attract new members by designing messages for impressionable youngsters who have the greatest exposure to digital messages.

It is useful to begin with an understanding of hate groups. In a 2003 article that appeared in the *FBI Law Enforcement Bulletin*, hate groups are described as groups that "[f]orm identities through symbols, rituals, and mythologies, which enhance the members' status and, at the same time, degrade the object of their hate." In the period between World Wars I and II, the German political party called the National Socialist Party (Nazi) emerged as one of the most successful hate groups. The party built itself on promoting what its members believed was the ideal race, degrading and excluding anyone who did not fit into this philosophy. The Nazis projected their hate on Jews and other miniority groups, building support with incendiary language and images. This group was also extremely successful in spreading its message of hate.

Adolf Hitler used his oratory skills to deliver many speeches to party members, constantly emphasizing his party's beliefs to generate hatred toward Jews. The Nazis also used efficient methods of propaganda to spread the hate message using posters, speeches, and other media messages. This was coordinated by Joseph Goebbels, the minister of Public Enlightenment and Propaganda during the Nazi regime from 1933 to 1945. The Nazi party created powerful messages to convince the German public that the Jews were responsible for all of Germany's misfortunes and to encourage people to act out against the Jews. This is a common strategy for groups like the Nazi party, since they use their message of hate to convey their beliefs to listeners and to attract them to join the party. This is often done by the use of powerful visual messages, as in the case of the Nazi regime in Germany, which used derogatory images of Jews in order to help spread its hateful message. The Nazis also developed specific icons like the swastika, a sacred symbol of some Eastern religions, that became revered symbols providing a center around which the hate group would grow.

Most hate groups continue to use the strategy that was well developed by the Nazis: creating an attractive message that would help them spread their word. Along with that, the groups have specific recruitment messages that would bring more people within their folds. Groups like al Qaeda spread their hate messages to impoverished Muslim youth in countries like Afghanistan, usually at religious schools where they are able to recruit members. These new members are then constantly exposed to al Qaeda's beliefs, encouraging them to become dedicated followers to the extent that they are willing to give up their own lives for the philosophy of the hate group.

These groups can use only a limited set of means to spread their message, unless they are backed by a government, as in the case of the Nazi party of Germany in the 1930s or al Qaeda in Afghanistan in the late 1990s. Other hate groups that do not have governmental backing depend on primitive means of propaganda that are usually restricted to a small region. For example, even with government backing, the bulk of the Nazi message was initially limited to Germany and parts of Austria. The message of fundamentalist Islamic groups was also largely limited to parts of the Middle East and Muslim countries. Groups that are not supported by larger organizations are usually unable to produce attractive and professionally produced propaganda, having to depend on amateur media technologies that do not result in very persuasive messages. An unattractive message does not do a good job of recruitment. The barriers of geography are overcome when digital methods are used for the propaganda, and the digital tools also allow amateurs to create attractive messages.

DIGITAL PROPAGANDA OF HATE

The process of digitization converts a message to binary data. Many different kinds of information, including sound, pictures, and texts, can be converted to a standardized format made up of zeroes and ones that are stored as bits of information. Different types of digital equipment such as a digital camera, a computer word processor, and a digital sound recorder all convert material to the digital bits. Once the bits are created, they can be stored in a computer file that can be copied many times without any loss of quality. It costs very little to make copies, since these files only take up space on a computer hard drive. The digital copies can then be easily transported, either on hard drives or as files attached to e-mails, and distributed over the Internet.

The Internet is composed of millions of computers that can exchange information, making it possible for anyone connected to the Internet to receive information from any other computer connected to the network. The information can be downloaded from Web-based computers that store digital files on publicly available networked computers, or the information can be broadcast to specific people through e-mail. A user can use the computer monitor to display the information contained in the file without any physical object such as a letter, poster, or artifact being sent to anyone. The entire transaction of information happens with digital files.

The various advantages provided by the use of computer networks to exchange virtual information makes digital propaganda an attractive option for hate groups. Digital information can be sent out to a very large audience at a low cost, and it is relatively easy to place digital material on a Web site once the initial promotional material has been created. It is also fairly easy to create an appealing design that can serve as an effective recruiting tool. These factors have led to tremendous growth in the number of hate group Web sites, with nearly 4,000 such sites reported in 2004 by the Simon Wiesenthal Center, which has been tracking hate Web sites for many years.

It is relatively difficult to control the operation of digital hate propaganda, another factor that makes it an attractive tool for hatemongers. The digital hate files can be kept on private machines that are difficult to track down. The many different kinds of mobile communication devices, along with the global reach of the Internet, also makes some hate groups essentially immune from the law, since the groups can set up their computers anywhere in the globe and make their message available worldwide. Legal immunity is then possible because a particular group might be considered a hate group in one part of the world but heroic in another part of the world. In this way, such groups can find safe havens through the use of the Internet. Once information has been digitized, it also becomes very difficult for outside parties to control its distribution, and the groups utilize this open-ended potential of digital data to spread their message. The widespread reach of the message also makes it easier for hate groups to vastly expand the places where they can find new recruits.

RECRUITING PEOPLE USING DIGITAL MESSAGES

In Hitler's Germany the Nazis recruited young Germans, as young as 12 years old, into Hitler Youth groups and used Nazi propaganda to train them to later join the Nazi Party as adults. Such recruiting was easy, since it was supported by the Nazi government. Most hate groups, however, do not have the support of other, larger organizations or institutions and must use alternate means for recruiting people. These methods have largely been restricted to a regional area and have depended mostly on printed media, such as books and pamphlets, that can be secretly distributed out of sight of law enforcement agencies. In 2002, *The Washington Post* reported that a local chapter of a hate group, the National Alliance, was using leaflets as a recruitment tool in parts of Virginia. The pamphlets were found stuck under car windshield wipers when community members returned to their cars after a town hall meeting. Canadian *Media Awareness Network* reports that such recruitment methods have been primarily used to target young people and "[h]ate groups have had to approach this group with their message by distributing pamphlets on school grounds and in neighborhood mailboxes." These same groups that publish their views on paper now supplement their leaflets with the more efficient digital recruitment methods.

Digital methods allow the hate groups to use tools that can appear more attractive and reach more people than amateurish pamphlets. Hate groups were quick to realize the strength of the Web in communicating with large audiences, and numerous groups established a Web presence through other Web sites, forums, and chat rooms. Although there is a lack of reliable research on the number of hate groups on the Internet, estimates range from a few hundred to thousands.

(continues on page 34)

HATE GROUPS

In America, a significant portion of hate groups are supremacist groups that advance a philosophy promoting the white race as the master race. These groups draw from a system of beliefs that consider all non-white people to be subhuman, which calls for the unification of the white race against all non-whites. This message often has a sympathetic audience of white youngsters who might want to find a sense of belonging to a group.

Many of these groups existed long before the development of

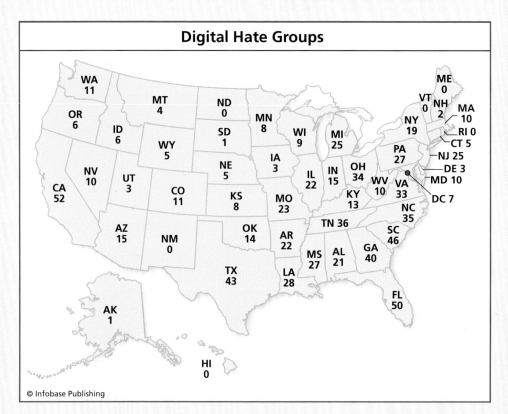

Digital Hate Groups

WA 11
MT 4
ND 0
MN 8
ME 0
VT 0
NH 2
MA 10
OR 6
ID 6
SD 1
WI 9
MI 25
NY 19
RI 0
CT 5
WY 5
IA 3
PA 27
NJ 25
NV 10
UT 3
NE 5
IL 22
IN 15
OH 34
WV 10
VA 33
DE 3
MD 10
CA 52
CO 11
KS 8
MO 23
KY 13
DC 7
AZ 15
NM 0
OK 14
AR 22
TN 36
NC 35
SC 46
TX 43
LA 28
MS 27
AL 21
GA 40
FL 50
AK 1
HI 0

© Infobase Publishing

There are numerous digital hate groups distributed across the United States with the larger states having larger number of such groups. It is very difficult to get an accurate count of such groups, but this chart cites the number of hate groups in each state, as indicated from printed materials and the digital presence of such groups.

the Internet. For example, the best-known supremacist group, the Ku Klux Klan (KKK), was formed in 1865 in Pulaski, Tennessee. Although the KKK has had its ups and downs through the past century, the Internet has allowed different segments of the KKK to find a common digital home. Here, the different KKK groups have set up Web sites like "Imperial Klans of America, Realm of Iowa," connecting the different subgroups together on the Internet. This has been the primary advantage provided by the Web: It has allowed geographically disconnected subgroups to come together in the virtual worldwide cyberspace.

The virtual space of the Internet has made it difficult for authorities to regulate these groups' activities in cyberspace. This is a problem that some countries are starting to face. For example, there are strict laws against hate groups in some European countries, but it is difficult to enforce the laws when the hate groups operate on the Internet. As *The Washington Post* reported in 2000, "German neo-Nazis don't need to leave their country to post their material; they can do it sitting at keyboards in Germany and transferring their material to Internet host computers in the United States." In such situations, the German government has to find ways to prosecute people who are using the Internet from a different country and could be protected by the laws of the country from which they operate. Since hate groups are spread out worldwide, it is difficult to control their operation if local laws do not allow interference. For example, there are fundamentalist religious groups like al Qaeda that promote violence toward people of other religions. In some cases, such messages are endorsed by national governments. This can make it impossible to control a specific group without entering into a conflict with the country that might be implicitly supporting the beliefs of the hate group. At those moments, the difference between a hate group and a country becomes difficult to judge. In a 2006 report about the educational system in Saudi Arabia, National Public Radio (NPR) reported that a group discovered in Saudi Arabian schools, "textbooks reflect an ideology of hatred against the other, against Christians, Jews other Muslims, for instance, Shiites and the majority Sunni Muslims and all others," who do not adhere to the interpretation

(continues)

(continued)
of Islam widely used in the country. Such educational systems encourage bigotry that can eventually turn into violent acts like the attack on the World Trade Center in New York in 2001, when Muslim fundamentalists, many of them educated in Saudi Arabia, carried out suicide attacks that caused the deaths of thousands.

Transferring hate to the digital realm has made it easier for these groups to thrive. Eventually, new methods need to be developed to control the way in which hate groups are able to mobilize the Internet for their dangerous causes.

(continued from page 31)

The Web site has become a particularly effective tool in recruitment, as many groups can advertise or promote their beliefs freely on the Internet while providing members with a forum full of like-minded people. This leads to discussions in which the hardcore members of the hate groups are able to discuss their philosophies and enter into dialogues with potential members. Such discussions can eventually become a way to attract people to the groups, as it is a more direct and efficient way for the leaders of such organizations to communicate with potential recruits. These Web sites also allow the groups to go beyond using written text as recruitment material, as recruiters can combine the written word with music, images, and other message forms.

Hate groups also try to attract people by using music that can be digitally distributed. Digitizing music is a fairly simple process and the digital file can be easily downloaded, or copied onto another computer, from the Web or be sent directly to users as attachments to e-mails. Digital hate music can become an effective way to spread the word of the hate group and to recruit new members. In a 2001 press release, the Anti-Defamation League, a group that monitors hate activities, reported: "Racist and anti-Semitic rock music is now a major recruitment tool and source of funding for hate groups. Many hate group members, especially neo-Nazi skinheads, have been drawn to white supremacy by listening to hate rock on the Internet."

Digital games also play a similar role in attracting people to hate groups. Younger computer users often spend a significant amount of time playing violent computer games. Hate groups have been able to use this fact to spread their word by creating games that depict the victim as the member of a hated group. For example, in 2002, Julia Scheeres of *Wired* magazine commented about hate games, writing that "The objective of these first-person shooters are predictably similar—to kill as many non-whites, Jews and everyone else they hate as possible." These multiplayer games allow people with similar hate-related philosophies to play together by teaming up to virtually kill members of the race that they hate, helping them distribute their message to potential recruits. Because many of these games are offered free to the players, they are attractive to kids who are interested in playing games but are unable to purchase them.

Digital technology allows anyone, including these hate groups, to use every multimedia tool available to create a memorable and entertaining Web site. Because Internet users will often revisit sites that focus on their interests and frequently update with new information, many hate groups will create Web pages that employ as many Internet tools as possible. Hate groups are then guaranteed that frequent viewers of their Web sites will hear or read their beliefs over and over again, which can eventually convince a viewer that the ideas being pushed by the Web site are his or her own opinions as well.

GOING BEYOND WEB SITES

In 2005, the Southern Poverty Law Center published an article in its magazine, *Intelligence Report,* about Stormfront, the first Neo-Nazi Web site. The article stated: "As pointed out by Cass Sunstein, the University of Chicago law professor who wrote the 2001 book *republic.com,* 'Extremists and hate-filled sites tend to attract likeminded people who, if isolated, could come to their senses.' Likeminded people talking to one another, Sunstein says, 'tend to become more extremist.'"

RECRUITMENT MESSAGES

Offering friendship is the most important theme in the Web-based recruitment messages of hate groups. Visually appealing Web sites are designed to offer a connection with a group of people who appear to be friendly and share a particular race, religion, or other feature. This commonality offers that group of people a sense of belonging; this feeling is furthered by claims that fellow members have been wronged in some way or are being threatened by other groups. For example, in one of the digital pamphlets of the white supremacist group called Aryan Nations, the group states, "The White race faces extinction now!" The statement is juxtaposed with the claim that Jewish people are out to destroy white America, then invites people to join the Aryan Nations movement. This is made particularly clear in the opening page of the Aryan Nations Web site, which states, "Violence solves everything" and then offers a link to a Web-based discussion forum. Visitors to the Web site can join the forum after registering themselves with a password.

The Web site also emphasizes the idea of pan-Aryanism, or the

Stormfront, whose motto is "White Pride Worldwide," began initially as a bulletin board, an early version of the Internet forum, and has evolved into one of the biggest hate-based cyber communities on the Internet. Created in 1995, this Web site began to gain momentum when the Internet became accessible to ordinary U.S. citizens and people began to log on to share their ideas and views. For the first time, hate groups and potential members of these groups across the nation were able to find a place where they could comfortably share their opinions without ridicule or opponents, while also finding others who agree with them.

The process of coming together is also facilitated by the use of another Internet tool called the Web log, or blog. A blog is a Web ability of the movement to cross traditional geographic boundaries. Before the Internet, much of the recruiting was conducted through word-of-mouth publicity, requiring the groups to recruit in restricted geographic areas. That burden on recruitment has now been removed, since the Web-based community exists in cyberspace, and anyone with access to the Web site can become a part of the Aryan movement. The new recruits can operate on their own, while remaining connected with other members by using the Web site as the main form of communication. The authors of these Web sites understand the power of this new tool and make claims such as "Aryan brothers and sisters across the globe, wherever they rest their heads, if in agreement with the principles and position of violent, pan-Aryan revolution against the jew [sic] are a part of the Aryan Nations." Without the Internet, a statement of international unity from the Aryan Nations would be hollow; because they are able to spread their message through the Web, the members of this group, along with other white supremacists, can easily gather more worldwide support. This shift could add power to the groups that spread hate toward others.

site that essentially works as an online journal where a writer can publish brief entries on whatever subject he or she wishes to cover. Web log authors, called bloggers, use their blogs to present their ideas on the Internet for everyone to see. Anyone with access to the Web can read the blog and respond to it. These messages serve as effective hate group recruiting tools, since people can become attracted to the messages or views featured in a blog. That can lead to a reader eventually becoming a member of the specific hate group. By its very nature, the content of the blog is less formal than the prepackaged and well-designed Web site because it is essentially just one person's thoughts, but this informality helps establish personal relationships among members of hate groups.

Although most of the relationships formed on these Web sites remain virtual, there are a few that have the potential to become a real-life threat to others. In September 2009, the Federal Bureau of Investigation (FBI) arrested Hosam Maher Husein Smadi, a Jordanian citizen studying in the United States, for attempting to blow up a Dallas, Texas, skyscraper. Smadi, apparently, was brought to the attention of the FBI after comments he made on a Muslim extremist Web site. Because international and national terrorists can connect and plan violent attacks on the Internet, the FBI has increased efforts to monitor specific Web sites in order to detect potential enemies or criminals.

The Internet has allowed members of hate groups to come together in a more intimate fashion than before. The many communication tools available on the Internet allow hate group members to create virtual communities that overcome traditional spatial boundaries. The members of the groups can exchange ideas just like members of any other Internet-based community, making the hate groups more effective than ever. Effective use of the digital tools can make the groups a more significant threat.

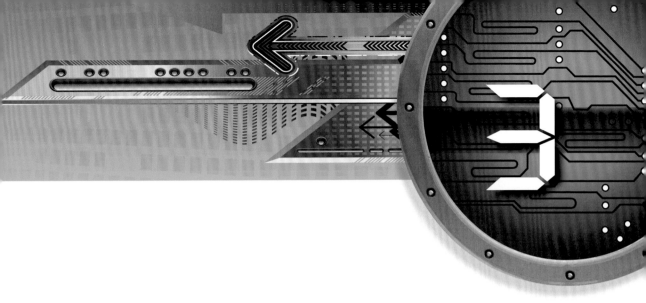

Viruses

The word *virus* has its origins in biology, where it refers to a microorganism that is smaller than bacteria. The Internet-based medical dictionary MedicineNet says that the virus "invades living cells and uses their chemical machinery to keep itself alive and to replicate itself." The key characteristic of the virus is that it can not survive by itself but requires a living cell as its human or animal host. Once in the cell, the virus can spread easily to other cells, and the person carrying the virus can transmit it to other people. The common cold is one of the best examples of a virus: A person can spread this virus, like all other viruses, by shaking hands with another person; thus the virus from the hand of an infected person can pass to the hand of a healthy person. The virus can then enter the healthy person's body if the person touches his or her eyes, mouth, or nose. Before long, many people may get infected by the virus, which can wreak havoc on large organisms. There are computer programs that are able to do the same thing to computers.

Virus programs were developed in the early days of computing, when the basic personal computer was introduced in the 1980s. These programs were written by students who were experimenting with new kinds of simple computer programs that would be powerful enough to have an effect on the operation of a computer. In the days before the Internet and large networks of computers, computer enthusiasts shared their new programs with their friends on a floppy disk—a flexible piece of plastic about the size of a slice of cheese. Mischievous programmers would create new games or interesting programs for their friends that would then direct their computers to perform tasks such as independently turning off or displaying a teasing message. These programs were innocent and confined to disks and individual computers—until someone discovered how to create a program that could independently clone and distribute itself to others.

The Washington Post staff writer Brian Krebs compiled a history of computer viruses and reported that the term was first used by a University of Southern California doctoral student, Fred Cohen, in 1983. Cohen explained that a virus can "affect other computer programs by modifying them in such a way as to include a (possibly evolved) copy of itself." This definition has been considered to capture the essential elements of a computer virus. Since the definition was developed before networked computers became popular, the definition does not emphasize the fact that the computer virus can also spread from one computer to the other using networks like the Internet. However, the ability of the virus to travel over the Internet is what makes it a particularly dangerous form of computer program. The possibility of spreading a virus arises from the fact that computers are connected to one another, allowing the machines to communicate with one another using networks. The communication involves the transmission of digital files that can hold a variety of information. The author of the virus program instructs the program to attach itself to legitimate files in order to move from one computer to another. Using the Internet, it is possible for a virus program to move rapidly, disrupting millions of computers very quickly. Sometimes computer users might be completely unaware that their machine has a virus since the virus is often disguised as a legitimate digital file. Users could inadvertently execute the commands in the file and damage their own computer as well as spread the file to other computers. Because people want to prevent their

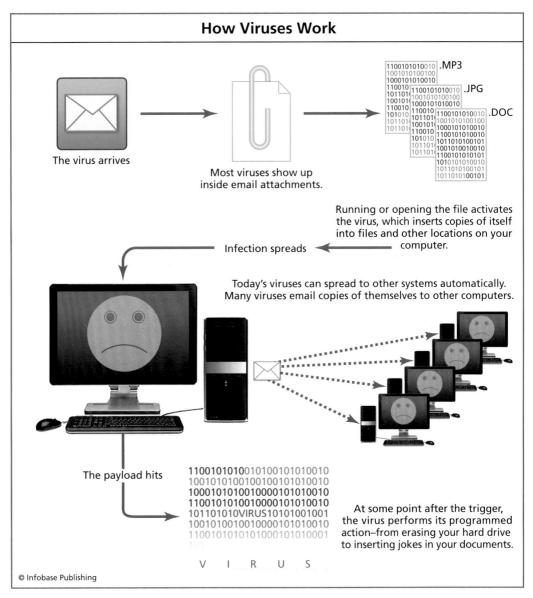

How Viruses Work

The virus arrives

Most viruses show up inside email attachments.

.MP3
.JPG
.DOC

Running or opening the file activates the virus, which inserts copies of itself into files and other locations on your computer.

Infection spreads

Today's viruses can spread to other systems automatically. Many viruses email copies of themselves to other computers.

The payload hits

At some point after the trigger, the virus performs its programmed action–from erasing your hard drive to inserting jokes in your documents.

V   I   R   U   S

© Infobase Publishing

A computer virus is a digital data file that is sent to a computer. The user would have to trigger the virus by opening the file, which then carries out a series of actions on the computer that not only damages the data on the computer but also sends the virus data file to other computers, continuing the cycle.

own computers from becoming infected with viruses, which could potentially affect all the computers of their friends, many invest in antivirus programs. In the first quarter of 2007, Symantec, a company that sells protection against computer viruses, reported sales of $1.4 billion, demonstrating the popularity of its Norton computer program that helps to keep a computer free of viruses.

CONTENT OF VIRUSES

A computer virus is not very different from many other computer program files that are made up of a series of instructions given to a computer. The instructions are created by computer programmers who develop a series of commands for the computer. There are special languages that are used to write the commands that the computer follows to do a series of tasks. Some of the tasks that the computer does are invisible to the user. For example, the computer must constantly monitor the amount of memory being used when multiple computer programs are running simultaneously to ensure that all the programs are operating as smoothly as possible. The user would not see how the computer monitors the memory, since that program runs in the background without disrupting the work that the user is doing, but these are programs that are essential for the operation of the computer. Virus programs often fall into the category of programs that run in the background, staying out of sight of the user.

A virus program is usually inconspicuous, since the virus file would be deleted if an average computer user could easily identify the file. This is why many virus files are attached to other kinds of files, like audio or image files, so that users will unknowingly allow the files to enter their computer. The virus file is also made up of a set of instructions that are designed to harm the computer. These instruct the electronic circuits in the computer to perform in a specific way. It is important to note that computers are made up of microprocessors with millions of electronic switches that are activated based on the instructions provided in a computer program. Although these switches will follow the directions of a computer program, they do not know or understand the consequences of their actions. A computer will, therefore, follow the instructions contained in a virus file in exactly the same way it would follow instructions in any other computer program, but the instructions in the virus file can actually damage the operations of the computer. One of the key instructions in most virus files tells the computer to make many copies of itself, which are then sent out attached to e-mails. These instructions allow the virus to spread over a network, and once the virus file reaches a new computer, it makes that computer follow the same set of instructions so that it can continue to damage computers while reproducing itself and infecting other machines. A virus program needs to have all of these characteristics to operate as a virus, and the programs are created by people who are often quite skilled in writing computer programs.

CREATING VIRUSES

The process of creating a virus is not very different from writing any other computer program, and popular programming languages like JavaScript can be used to create viruses. Any skilled programmer is able to easily author a virus; some viruses have been written by people as young as 13 years old. The creation of a virus does not require many special tools, making it possible to create a virus on a mediocre computer. Most of the programming languages required to write a virus are available for creating legitimate programs, and there are numerous books that teach how to write programs using these languages. Once a virus has been written, it can also be easily uploaded to the Internet. Thereafter, the virus can spread by itself by attaching to legitimate files. The author of the virus can simply send an e-mail to one person with the virus file and that e-mail can then reproduce and spread itself all over the Internet. As pointed out by Monte Enbysk, lead editor of Microsoft.com, "Virus writers are generally younger (some as young as 10 or 11 years old), on a lower rung of the underground tech strata [hierarchy]." What is more important to understand are the reasons why people would want to spread malicious programs.

Sarah Gordon, an international specialist who studies the profile of virus writers at the IBM Thomas J. Watson Research Center, suggests that those who write viruses are people who have a rebellious, antisocial streak. At the same time, Gordon's research shows large variation in what the writers consider to be ethically wrong. Some of the writers do not exhibit any other antisocial behavior other than writing viruses. It is, therefore, not just a desire to be malicious that motivates the author of a virus but also an interest in simply doing something new. Most virus writers have a strong creative tendency, one that is satisfied when developing novel uses of the computer. For example, one virus writer was quoted in a *Rolling Stone* magazine article saying, "I found it fascinating that I could actually make this computer do what I wanted." What seems to motivate the virus writers is the desire to control the computer, combined with the sense of power achieved from doing this. The virus writer often loses sight of the fact that the virus can really harm someone, downplaying the consequences of his or her malicious work.

The writer of a virus is also not located in any specific geographic location. Viruses can be written anywhere to be sent out over the Internet. One of the early viruses called "The Brain" was produced by computer programmers in Pakistan in 1986. The virus spread to many computers over the Internet, which, at that time, was still in its early, primitive stages. The ability to create and spread viruses from anywhere in the world makes it particularly difficult to catch virus authors, since the laws of one country cannot be applied to a person in a different country, even though the Internet crosses national boundaries. This makes a large number of people very easily vulnerable to viruses.

VULNERABILITY TO VIRUSES

Any computer or other digital device is vulnerable to virus attacks since a virus is a digital file. This means it can create problems for any digital gadget that would be able to follow the instructions contained in the virus. Once a digital gadget has received a virus file, the gadget is liable to be controlled by the file. The digital gadget could be a computer, a cell phone, a personal digital assistant, or any similar device that is affected once the virus file has been placed in the memory of the device.

Virus files are often disguised or hidden, causing most devices to become infected, usually unknowingly, by the users themselves. Digital files are unable to enter a device unless a user has done something to allow the file to be recorded in the device's memory. Naturally, a user does not do this voluntarily but is tricked into allowing a virus digital file to enter the gadget. Because of this, one of the most common tricks is to attach a virus to another file, one of a popular or common format. The virus file enters the computer when a user copies what he or she believes is a legitimate file into the memory of the computer, simultaneously saving the virus. Thereafter, the legitimate file becomes the carrier of the virus, and the user can unknowingly send the carrier file to other users, who, when infected, will also not know they are helping spread the virus. This process makes users who frequently exchange legitimate files more vulnerable to virus attacks and more likely to spread viruses.

Shared networks like the Internet have made larger numbers of people vulnerable to virus attacks. Millions of people use the Internet for exchanging e-mail, which is one of the Internet's most common uses. The process of sending an e-mail involves the sharing of a digital file because the e-mail is nothing other than binary code that is sent from one computer to another. This makes an e-mail a good carrier for a virus file. This is particularly dangerous, since e-mails are often automatically stored in the memory of a user's computer when the computer is connected to the Internet. The user might not even realize that an e-mail containing a virus has embedded itself in the memory of the computer, and he or she would continue to use the computer unaware that the computer has an e-mail that contains a virus. The effect of viruses would have been far more profound if the e-mail itself operated as a virus file. However, in

(continues on page 48)

TYPES OF VIRUSES

Over the years, since the early 1980s, computer programmers have developed many different kinds of viruses, all of which have the common purpose of disrupting the normal functioning of a computer. Viruses are classified on the basis of the damage they do to the computer. In his 2005 book, *Computer Viruses: From Theory to Applications,* Eric Filiol offered a broad definition of a virus as a program that "discreetly installs itself in a data processing system, without users' knowledge or consent, with a view to either endangering data confidentiality, data integrity and system availability. "This definition

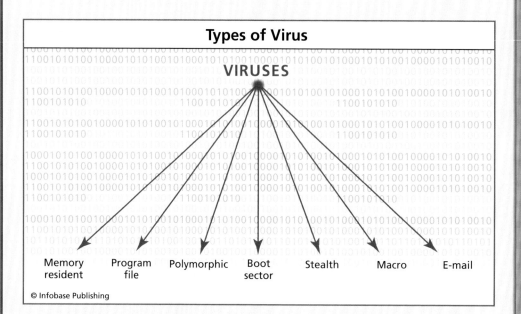

Types of Virus

VIRUSES

Memory resident — Program file — Polymorphic — Boot sector — Stealth — Macro — E-mail

© Infobase Publishing

A virus is a digital data file similar to any other computer program that can work on different elements of the computer. Some are designed to work only on the computer memory, others have many different characteristics, and some act on e-mail programs. All eventually interfere with the normal functioning of a computer.

suggests that viruses can do many different things to a computer.

Some viruses like the Code Red and Nimda, both of which were released in 2001, are designed to infiltrate a computer and make the contents of the computer visible to outsiders. These programs usually undermine the password protection of a computer, and the authors of the programs are able to peek into the hard drive of the infected computer when it is connected to the Internet. The user of the computer would be unaware of the way in which the data confidentiality has been compromised. These viruses not only disrupt the working of a specific computer by violating the protected data, but they can quickly spread to many computers, collectively disrupting data confidentiality, which can eventually stall the operation of the Internet. For example, when the Code Red virus first appeared in 2001, it affected nearly 250,000 computers in one day and slowed down data transmission on the Internet.

Other viruses are designed to destroy the data on a computer by violating the integrity of the data. This kind of virus was particularly popular in the early days of computing when large numbers of personal computers used to operate the Disk Operating System (DOS) software. This operating system stored some important information about the computer in a part of the hard drive called the boot sector, an area of the hard drive where the computer stores the important codes that are needed for basic computer operations such as starting up your computer or running ordinary programs. Malicious programs like Stoned would corrupt the data in the boot sector of the hard drive, which would cause the computer to malfunction. A similar virus called Michelangelo, named after the famous artist, struck in 1992 and was described by the news service of Stanford University as "[a]n especially destructive strain, [that] may erase parts of a user's hard drive. This can happen every March 6, which is the famous artist's birthday, according to security officials in the Stanford Data Center." The mischievousness of virus authors becomes evident when the viruses are supposed to become active on famous days to

(continues)

(continued)
coincide with some characteristic of the virus.

When a virus strikes a computer, it can harm saved information or become unable to function. Continuing to use the computer could easily help the spread of viruses if the computer is connected to a network or if files from the computer are transferred to another machine. A computer infected with a virus should be immediately isolated and preferably kept off the network until the virus files have been removed.

(continued from page 45)

most cases, viruses are sent as attachments to the e-mail. A typical e-mail with an attachment is made up of two separate digital files: The e-mail itself is digital data, and it is accompanied by the attached file, which also is digital data. The user has the choice of either deleting the attached file or storing it into the memory of his or her computer. The virus is allowed into the computer if the user accepts the attached file. After that, the virus can do its damage from inside the user's computer.

It is important to note that the way a computer user treats files coming from others has a large impact on how viruses operate. A computer that is not connected to the Internet is far less likely to be affected by a virus. Similarly, the way a computer is used impacts the vulnerability of the computer and its users. Those users who are unaware of the way in which viruses operate are far more likely to be affected by viruses. It has been demonstrated that users who are willing to copy files from unknown sources or accept attachments to e-mails from unknown senders have a greater chance of being affected by viruses. On the other hand, users who are cautious about accepting doubtful files are better protected from viruses. Unfortunately, it only requires a few vulnerable users to allow a virus file to spread, and once the virus file is able to move from one computer to another, it can cause a significant amount of damage to computer systems.

THE EFFECTS OF VIRUSES

A virus file is designed to make the computer perform in a way that would be harmful to itself. A computer is usually made up of a series of interconnected components such as the hard drive, the keyboard, the mouse, and the monitor. These different parts of the computer are operated by a series of instructions sent to the central processing unit, or CPU, of the computer. The virus files instruct the computer to do things that would disrupt the normal activities of the user, by damaging files that the user needs, or by disabling some of the critical parts of the computer.

A virus can erase useful files such as important documents. It instructs the computer to remove a set of files from its hard drive. Most computer files used by Windows-based computers have a file name that includes a suffix. This part of the file name is standardized for certain kinds of files; for example, most Microsoft Word document files have an extension ".doc" that tells the computer to treat the file in a specific way. A virus can direct a computer to delete all the files with a specific suffix or, in other cases, a virus might include instructions to alter useful files so that they can no longer be used. In such cases, the file is damaged to the extent that the user is unable to access the useful data in the file.

Some viruses give the computer instructions that would make the hardware of the computer unusable. There are not many instances of hardware being physically damaged by a virus file, but a virus can change the instructions the computer has stored to do specific tasks. Most computers have some permanent instructions included with them to ensure that they turn on correctly. Some of these instructions are placed on memory that is separate from the hard drive of the computer. A few viruses are able to change the instructions on the flash memory, which would make the computer unusable.

The main effect of the computer virus is lost productivity on the part of the user. A virus can make a computer unusable, forcing the user to repair the computer, and the repair process itself can lead to complete loss of all the data stored on the hard drive of the computer. A user who stores critical data on a computer could find it very difficult to recreate all the information once it has been lost. In this way, viruses can potentially destroy thousands of hours of work. Since viruses spread over the Internet, the damage could quickly spread to thousands of users and cripple all computer-based activities. It is quite possible that a virus could emerge that could completely disable the information technology system of a nation. This threat has led to the development of a series of strategies to ensure

WORMS AND TROJAN HORSES

The popularity of the Internet has given rise to a specific form of malicious computer program that is spread primarily through e-mails. These programs attach themselves to e-mails and then reside on the receiver's computer. Once residing on the computer, the primary task of the virus program is to use the e-mail address book of the host computer and send out e-mails with the virus to everyone in the address book. In this manner the program propagates itself over the Internet, and these computer programs are called worms. Worms are relatively benign and do not hurt the host computer, but the rapid reproduction and delivery of numerous e-mails could slow down the speed of data transmission on the Internet and disrupt the normal operation of e-mail. Every year, since the launching of the first known worm in 1988 by a student at Massachusetts Institute of Technology, new worm programs have threatened computers. Some of the worm programs have also morphed to look and act like viruses, since these programs not only jam up the data transmission on the Internet but also destroy the data on the host computer. For example, *PC World* magazine has rated a worm called LoveLetter, released in 2000, as the worst worm-virus combination in recent history. Frank Thorsberg of the magazine said, "LoveLetter is the worm everyone learned to hate in spring 2000. The infection affected that users are less vulnerable to virus attacks. There are several ways a user can protect himself or herself from viruses.

STOPPING VIRUSES

One of the ways in which viruses are stopped is with the use of computer programs that can detect viruses. Some of these programs are used by large institutions that receive a high number of e-mails. These programs check every single e-mail to ensure

millions of computers and caused more damage than any other computer virus to date." The program changed the content of critical programs and irreversibly altered the content of hard drives, which made it nearly impossible for the average user to retrieve the lost data.

While the worm works by itself, another kind of malicious program resides on the computer and needs to be activated by the user. These viruses are called Trojan horses because they mimic the legendary wooden horse of Greek mythology that secretly carried warriors into Troy. The warriors were only able to gain access to the inside of Troy, a walled city the ancient Greeks fought to enter for 10 years, when overconfident Trojan citizens brought the giant horse inside. When the Tro-

jans fell asleep, the Greek warriors attacked and burned the city to the ground. Similarly, the computer version of the Trojan horse might look innocuous, like a music file attached to an e-mail, but clicking on the music file could release the program, which would interfere with the normal use of the computer.

It is difficult to pinpoint a specific Trojan horse virus that has been most harmful, but all these programs rely on the computer user's curiosity to become operational. The person who receives a Trojan horse must actively open the file to get infected. These programs are unable to spread on their own, and they are also unable to replicate themselves, making them less likely to spread as widely as viruses and worms that move over the Internet.

that no virus files are included in the e-mails. Since most virus programs have specific kinds of binary code, there are ways of checking for these codes to detect virus files. The offensive files can be removed once the files are detected. This method is proving to be quite effective in controlling the movement of viruses over the Internet. All files have to pass through many different computers when going from one point to another on the Internet, and when all the different computers have virus detection software, it is quite likely that a virus file would be quickly detected. Even if one computer misses a virus, another computer might stop it. Some of these computer programs are loaded into computers that allow e-mail to enter an institution. Although this sometimes results in non-virus files being incorrectly tagged as virus files and therefore prevented from reaching their destination, it is safer to have virus protection that might stop a few good files than to have no virus protection at all.

There are some computer programs that can also be installed on individual personal computers that constantly watch out for potentially harmful files. These protection programs periodically look at all possible digital information that is stored in a computer and alert the user of any suspicious computer code. These virus detection programs check all files that enter the computer, including those that might be copied from a portable memory device like a flash drive. The protection programs can be easily updated to ensure that a computer is protected against the most recent virus files.

While computer programs are able to detect viruses, the user of a computer plays an important role in stopping viruses too. Most viruses are spread with the use of e-mail, and a slight alteration in the way users treat e-mails can help to stop the spread of viruses. As the Web site About.com, which provides tips on computer use, points out, "The simplest, most effective method to protect against email-borne threats involves the use of filtering software." These tools eliminate an e-mail containing a virus even before it reaches the user. On the other hand, a user who receives an e-mail with an attachment has unknowingly already started the process of virus

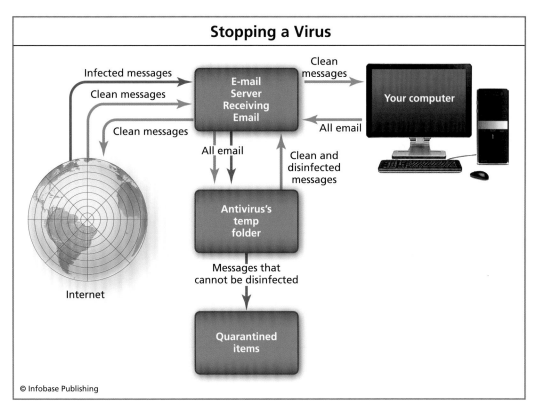

Stopping a Virus

Infected messages

Clean messages

Clean messages

Clean messages

All email

Clean messages

Your computer

All email

Clean and disinfected messages

E-mail Server Receiving Email

Antivirus's temp folder

Internet

Messages that cannot be disinfected

Quarantined items

© Infobase Publishing

Viruses are digital data files that have some special characteristics. It is possible to stop a virus file from entering a computer by setting up systems that are able to detect the special characteristics of virus files. When such files are detected they are first stored in a temporary memory of the computer and then finally stored in a part of the computer memory where they can remain quarantined and relatively harmless.

activation. This is why it is very important to be careful with files attached to e-mails. One of the best ways to stop viruses is to be cautious with e-mails from unknown senders, and it is a good practice to not attempt to open or view files that are sent by strangers. Every user has a set of known people with whom e-mail communication takes place, and those people, who are known to the user, are less likely to send a virus-laden e-mail. Users should also keep virus detection software like Norton AntiVirus on their computers, as such programs can provide significant protection against infection by a virus. These programs also ensure that viruses are not inadvertently reproduced. Protection against viruses requires keeping a machine free of viruses as well as ensuring that viruses are not accidentally sent out of a machine.

The main way to reduce the spread of viruses is for users to be responsible computer and Internet users. Even with all the protection, viruses can still cause problems. Since viruses can damage needed data files, it is also important for users to protect the digital information saved on their computer. Backing up files frequently is a good way to ensure their safety. The user of every individual computer is the person who can best defend against virus attacks.

Cyber Terrorism

In 2001, a disgruntled person who was refused a full-time job with the Maroochy Shire government in Queensland, Australia, used a computer program along with some other electronic equipment to gain access to the water control system of the region. He then released 264,172 gallons (1 million liters) of raw sewage into the local rivers. As a result, "[m]arine life died, the water turned black, and the stench was unbearable to local residents," said Janelle Bryant of the Australian Environmental Protection Agency. An incident like this can be considered an example of terrorism in the digital age: using digital tools and computer systems to carry out violent, threatening, or destructive acts. In the digital age, a disrupted computer system could compromise national and personal security, putting financial or personal information of a country or an individual at risk.

The primary goal of terrorism is to strike fear into the hearts of others. Terrorist acts are often done by those who consider themselves to be less powerful than those they target. Small groups of people are able to cause severe damage to large communities by a few evil deeds. This is what happened on September 11, 2001, when members of the al Qaeda terrorist organization hijacked four airplanes; the planes crashed into the Pentagon, partially destroying the structure, and two planes collided with the towers of the World Trade Center, causing the buildings to collapse. The last plane crash-landed in a field in Pennsylvania. Nearly 3,000 people were killed in this coordinated attack.

Those who want to use the tactics of terror as their primary means of communication also have to rely on surprising their victims, as in the case of the September 11 attacks. An act of terror is most effective when it comes without warning. Those who want to frighten people also generally do not care about their victims. In a time of war, soldiers fight other soldiers; civilians are usually not targets of military attacks. Those who are interested in committing acts of terror, however, often prefer to attack civilian targets in order to increase the level of fear in the public. The victims of terrorist acts are usually civilians who have no way to protect themselves against the terrorists, and even a single person can easily kill a large number of people. In the case of the 1995 Oklahoma City bombing, only two terrorists connected with anti-government militia in the United States bombed the Alfred P. Murray Federal Building, killing 168 people and destroying the building.

Acts of terror also aim to disrupt normal, everyday life. Even when two countries are in a state of war with each other, there could be relative calm at times for civilians. Life could go on with some sense of normalcy once everyone comes to terms with the fact that life during a war is different from normal life. Indeed, there is an expectation that some things will be different when countries are at war with each other. For example, during World War II the German air force, also known as the Luftwaffe, bombed London almost constantly for a period of nearly a year starting in September 1940. This disrupted life in the city, but people were prepared for the attacks, and the city developed a way of coping with the bombing:

it offered the train stations of the underground rail network as bomb shelters. City officials were able to manage the disruption since they knew that the bombings would be occurring daily. Acts of terror, on the other hand, create unmanageable disruption, because the unexpected attacks can drastically change everyday life for millions of people. Some victims' lives may even be changed forever once a terrorist act has happened. For example, the attack on the World Trade Center in 2001 not only led to loss of life at the site of the attack, but it also disrupted the lives of Americans for a long period of time. The immediate effect was the complete shutdown of all air transportation in the United States, leading to nationwide chaos as well as long-term financial effects on the airline industries. This type of fallout continued for many years as normal systems were disrupted by the attack. Digital terrorist attacks, such as spam or hacking, are unlikely to result in the loss of life, but they can similarly disrupt and create unease in everyday life.

SHUTTING DOWN CRITICAL COMPUTER SYSTEMS

Some believe that terrorist attacks involving computers would not be that catastrophic. In 2002, *Washington Monthly* writer Joshua Green wrote, "There is no such thing as cyberterrorism—no instance of anyone ever having been killed by a terrorist (or anyone else) using a computer." This statement is true. It is unlikely that a group of terrorists would be able to cause direct physical harm by a computer-based attack, but that does not take away a threat of terrorists causing harm by attacking the large amounts of data that are stored as digital files on millions of computers. The goal of terrorism is to disrupt a normal working system by creating a chaotic condition, which can be achieved through computer systems.

Computers play a significant role in data storage, and plenty of sensitive personal and institutional information is stored as digital data. Some of this information is of critical value for national security. There are three ways in which terrorists can target this data:

Using tools like viruses, they could destroy some of the data, and it might take some time for institutions to restore this data from backed-up resources. The destruction of critical data can lead to widespread chaos, even if it disappears for only a short period of time. On a smaller scale, this would be similar to a computer crash, which leaves the user temporarily unable to access the stored information on the computer. This is similar to the ways in which the 2001 attacks on the World Trade Center resulted in long-lasting financial woes for some industries. That same effect can be produced if terrorists are able to destroy critical data.

Another way in which terrorists can use data is by gaining access to sensitive information. Most computer systems are adequately protected against digital intrusion, but terrorists can access data if there is a weakness in the digital defenses. Such access might remain undetected for a long time, and the terrorist can then monitor the sensitive information that is stored in the computer system, which can then be used to plan other terror activities. This is similar to the process of spying that is used in war; the side that has greater information about the enemy's plans has a greater chance of winning the war. In this way, access to digital information can provide some advantage in real life.

Interfering with common computer-based communication is another way in which terrorists can disrupt everyday life. The computer has become a key component of many communication networks, including the Internet and telephone systems, both including hard-wired and wireless (cellular) systems. Terror attacks can target these communication systems by overloading the computer networks with data. Terrorists can flood the network with useless data to disrupt the flow of useful data. Such attacks can cripple the way a nation responds to other attacks of terror, because people become vulnerable if they are unable to communicate with one another. Such conditions can spread panic to help the terrorists reach their goal of disrupting a normal system. Terrorists who operate in the digital realm can end up compromising national security by disrupting the normal flow of information.

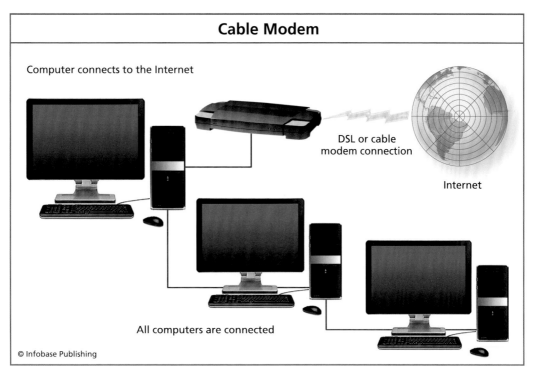

Cable Modem

Computer connects to the Internet

DSL or cable modem connection

Internet

All computers are connected

© Infobase Publishing

A device called a modem can be used to connect a series of computers to the Internet using the television cable that has become commonplace in many parts of the World. At the same time, the cable modem can become a vulnerable part of a network since a significant amount of information is channeled through this gadget.

Many everyday activities of people and institutions revolve around financial exchanges, ranging from individual uses of Internet-based banking systems to the way in which large institutions exchange financial information over computer networks. This creates a dependancy on these conveniences and the possible crippling of these exchanges if financial information became the target of terrorist attacks.

ACCESSING INFORMATION

Most financial transactions involve computers, since almost all financial data is stored as digital files that are sent from one computer to

HACKING

Hacking refers to the process by which a computer programmer is able to access files on a computer that contains sensitive information not meant for public use. Data that is protected from public access is usually secured with passwords and other barriers that are meant to discourage unauthorized use of the information. Only those who have access to the password are supposed to view the data, and the hacking process can usually find a way past data protection, which allows the hacker to see and modify the data. Hacking started in the early 1960s on university campuses, where creative students who wanted to test the limits of a comput-er's power experimented with large interconnected computers. The process of testing computers evolved into more malicious activities by the 1980s, when hacker groups started to break into computer systems. The Milwaukee-based group called 414, which was able to access private data on numerous computers, is an example of such groups.

The process of hacking begins with locating a weak point in the security system of a computer. Machines that are connected to the Internet need to be able to exchange legitimate digital data. Hackers are able to find the way in which the data is exchanged and then seek weaknesses with the computer programs

another over various communication networks. Also, most information is digitized to be stored on computer disks and hard drives. Anyone who can access that memory can also access the data, and terrorists can use that information to cause harm.

As mentioned in Chapter One, those with access can terrorize an individual or a group whose confidential data has been made vulnerable to others. This is not an act of terror as in the case of a group of people blowing up a building, but misuse of someone's personal data can cause him or her significant distress—and that makes the person a victim of a personal terror attack. Identity theft is the that guard the data entry and exit points. After locating the weakness, hackers are able to access the data on the targeted computer. The purpose of the access can be to simply see the data, or it can be as bold as to change the data in a noticeable manner. For example, in 1999, hackers protesting the accidental bombing of the Chinese Embassy in Belgrade were able to break into the computer systems of U.S. government agencies and alter the content of Web sites. Reporting on the incident, CNN.com noted that "[t]he hackers planted messages condemning the bombing on the main Web sites of the Energy and Interior Departments and the National Park Service."

Dedicated hackers are able to get past security systems and, in some cases, can do even more damage than altering Web site content. Hackers can infiltrate critical national services such as the electricity generation and distribution system and completely disrupt everyday life. This is what happened in 2007 when two engineers hacked into the traffic control system of Los Angeles and created widespread traffic jams at some of the major intersections. The *San Diego Times* reported that, "While the traffic congestion did not lead to injuries, it took four days for officials with the city's Automated Traffic Surveillance and Control Center to undo the damage." As more systems become dependent on networked computers, it is likely that incidents like this could become commonplace.

primary example of this type of information misuse. Individuals in most nations have an identification number that connects a real person to the digital information about himself or herself. Obtaining the identity number allows access to data about the person that can be misused by people wanting to cause harm.

In the United States, the identity number is known as the Social Security number. In Britain people have a National Insurance number, just as people in India have the Permanent Account number. Most individuals also have other critical numbers that connect them to information databases. These numbers could

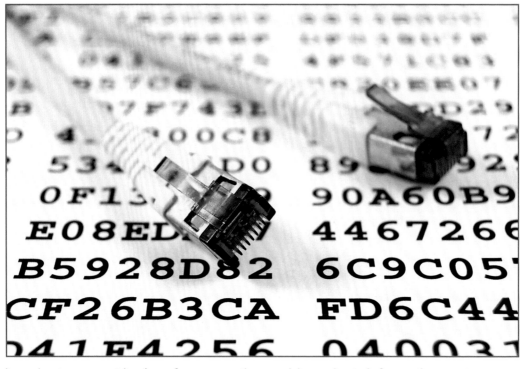

In order to prevent hackers from secretly acquiring private information sent over the Internet, many Web sites, particularly the ones involved in e-commerce, will use encryption methods to protect their customers. Binary code containing information like addresses, Social Security numbers, and credit card numbers are transformed into a jumble of confusion meant to deter and prevent identity theft.

include a passport number, bank account numbers, credit card numbers, driver's license numbers, and other identifiers. These numbers represent different pieces of information about a person, and among these, some numbers are more critical than others. For example, nearly every financial and governmental form in the United States asks for the Social Security number. This number is also tied to the credit rating that shows financial health of a person or a company. Most of the information is stored as digital data on numerous computers with no one monitoring how the data is used.

Social Security numbers and other identifying numbers are considered the keys that would allow access to personal digital data, which is why personal acts of terror involve misuse of personal digital information. A criminal can gain access to some of the key personal identification numbers, and, armed with those numbers, he or she can access an individual's personal information. This information can then be used to assume the identity of the person whose personal numbers have been stolen. After that, it is possible to easily use the false identity to do anything from applying for credit cards to withdrawing money from a bank account. In the case of misuse of credit cards, many criminals will borrow the maximum amount allowed on the card and then leave the bill unpaid. Often, these unpaid bills will remain on a person's permanent credit report until an investigation can clear the identity theft victim of wrongdoing. Although it is not the victim's responsibility to pay for these bills, the unpaid bills may still have permanent effects on the victim's finances, particularly when he or she applies for a loan or tries to purchase a house or car.

It is estimated that one in four homes in the United States was stuck by identity theft in 2003, and the number has gone up since then. Although these criminal acts against an individual might not bring the widespread panic related to mass, violent acts of terror, identity theft can be quite a terrifying experience for the victim. This is why most countries consider identity theft to be a criminal act, and there are laws to prosecute identity thieves. Unfortunately, it is often difficult to catch the thief because the theft of digital information can be done from outside national boundaries. For example, because thieves in one country can steal the identity of a person in another country, it is extremely difficult to enforce laws under such circumstances. At the same time, it is important for people to recognize the threat of identify theft and take steps to protect themselves against possible attacks.

PROTECTING PERSONAL INFORMATION

Protection of personal information begins with the recognition that most people essentially have a dual existence: as a person in real life and as a set of digital data. Most people are careful about protecting

(continues on page 66)

ENCRYPTION

Encryption is a process that is used to alter the content of a message in such a way that only the receiver and the sender of the message are able to read it. The process depends on inventions in the area of cryptography, which provides a system for hiding the content of a message. An encrypted message is made up of two parts. One part contains the message that would appear to be gibberish to someone who does not have the second part: the key to make sense of the gibberish. The key contains instructions about the way in which letters and symbols have been substituted so that the reader can use that information to make sense of the message. This method of encryption by letter substitution has been in use from the days of the Greek and Roman civilizations, when military messages were sent using methods of letter substitution. For example, the letters "gns bneedd" mean nothing until the key is provided; the key states that each letter of the original message has been substituted by the letter that appears before it in the alphabet. Once that key is known, the letter "g" becomes "h," and all the letters spell out "hot coffee."

It is difficult or impossible to know the exact word unless the substitution key is known. All encrypted messages need to be accompanied by the key so that the receiver can make sense of the message. However, the key has to be sent only once, and all coded messages are deciphered using the same key. This also means that if the key became known to others, the secrecy of the message would be lost. This process was used successfully during World War II, when the Germans were able to develop a machine called the Enigma that could encrypt and decrypt messages in a manner that became nearly impossible for the British and the Americans to understand (until they captured one of the machines) since there were numerous combinations of substitution produced by the machines.

Encryption in the digital age follows the principle of ancient encryption, but it offers a very large number of substitution systems that would be impossible to guess without having the key. One of the

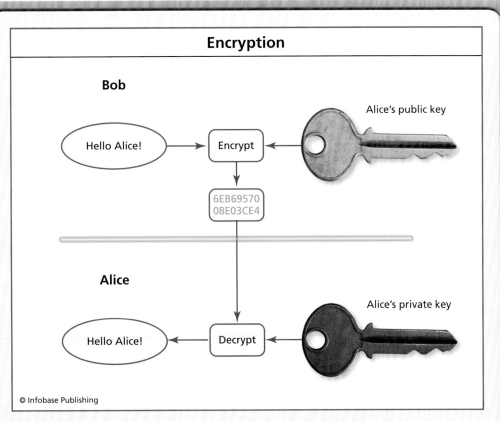

Encryption

Bob

Hello Alice! → Encrypt ← Alice's public key

6EB69570
08E03CE4

Alice

Hello Alice! ← Decrypt ← Alice's private key

© Infobase Publishing

Digital information can be altered in such a way that it would be impossible for an eavesdropper to decode the content. Only those who have the appropriate key can decipher the scrambled information that has been encrypted in a very specific way.

most common forms of encryption involves the use of the symmetric key, which uses the same set of instructions for the sender and the receiver. This is the simplest method of encryption but it is not the most efficient, as Susan Young and Dave Aitel point out in their 2004 book, *The Hacker's Handbook: The Strategy Behind Breaking Into and Defending Networks.* The authors write that "it is possible for a hacker to obtain the key" and use that for deciphering the message. Other methods pro-vide keys that are new for each com-

(continues)

(continued)

munication, which makes it more difficult to decipher the key and better protects the message. The ease with which encryption can be done to digital communication has led to greater adoption of the technology for most digital data transmission. For example, many Web sites have an address that starts with "https" as opposed to the traditional "http," where the additional "s" means that the data sent to the Web site is secure and encrypted. It is important to ensure that sensitive data is only transmitted over the Web when the "s" appears as a part of the Web site address. Encryption is a good way to protect data, but it must be consciously used to be effective.

(continued from page 63)

the real person, taking precautions such as locking the door in one's home and being mindful of surroundings when one is in an unfamiliar place. People do not usually leave their belongings unprotected or share sensitive information with strangers, and children are taught to be wary of people they do not know. Similar strategies need to be adopted to protect individuals' digital existence.

It is important to realize that most electronic transactions involve the exchange of private digital data. People need to be sure that such transactions are done in a secure fashion. The Internet has made it possible to share financial information very easily, with financial data transmitted whenever there is a purchase made using a Web site. When someone enters a credit card number into a Web site, that information may be at risk for theft. This makes it important to ensure that the information is sent using secure systems that involve a process called encryption. Coding the data in an encrypted fashion protects the credit card information from being accessed during the transaction. Many Web sites also require a password to access information on the Web sites. These passwords should be protected and updated periodically, since a patient thief can figure out passwords if they are not changed often. It is also important to know what personal digital data is stored on different computers. In the United States, most money-lending decisions are based on the credit-worthiness of the borrower, which is determined by a credit score that indicates the financial reliability of a person. Identity theft can artificially lower the credit score, which in turn can hurt the financial standing of an individual. Periodic checking of the score is one way to be aware of identity theft, which can be managed better if it is caught early.

It is also important to be careful about sharing information, since some identity thieves try to obtain sensitive personal information by posing as legitimate businesses or organizations. It is not uncommon for people to receive e-mails asking for sensitive personal information. These e-mails appear to come from legitimate sources like banks, but it is important to verify the authenticity of the sources. For example, in 2005, a virus was released with an e-mail that appeared to come from the FBI. As a result, the FBI Web site put out a disclaimer stating, "Recipients of this or similar solicitations should know that the FBI does not engage in the practice of sending unsolicited e-mails to the public in this manner." Because of such deceptive practices, it is unwise to disclose personal information without knowing for certain who is receiving it; many incidents of identity theft involve unknowing victims innocently sending information to untrustworthy sources. MSN.com, on its *Money* page, suggests: "Whenever anyone contacts you asking for private identity or financial information, make no response other than to find out who they are, what company they represent and the reason for the call." This is no different from being aware of whom one is dealing with in real life.

If an identity thief is caught, there are different ways of prosecuting him or her. Stealing information is considered a federal offense in the United States, and people who are caught stealing another person's identity can face stiff punishments. However, the thief can only be caught if victims realize and report the crime, so it is important to be vigilant about all activity involving your digital information. The best way to protect oneself is to be aware of the different ways in which the digital data can be misused and to constantly check to see if there has been any suspicious activity done in one's name. Protecting one's identity from thieves is somewhat like a spy operation: A person should assume that dishonest people could be spying on personal information and then make sure that the spy is unable to find any useful information. The process of digital spying can extend beyond individuals and identities and can be used by institutions and governments.

Digital Spying

I n 1994, the United States legislature signed into law the Communications Assistance for Law Enforcement Act (CALEA). This allowed the federal government to work with the private telecommunication companies in America to "preserve the ability of law enforcement agencies to conduct electronic surveillance by requiring that telecommunications carriers and manufacturers of telecommunications equipment modify and design their equipment, facilities, and services to ensure that they have the necessary surveillance capabilities." Since then, there have been many technological developments and political events that have led to the enforcement of the CALEA, so that the government could use technological means to maintain surveillance of sensitive information critical to national security. This chapter focuses on the way information is tracked in the digital age. The chapter specifically examines how messages exchanged between people can be monitored, since many of the exchanges happen digitally, using existing technologies like satellite communication. The chapter also considers the role of other spying methods such as the use of space-based imaging of the globe and the development of elaborate, interconnected databases that would produce a very detailed description of an individual or group.

One of the primary goals of spying is secretly collecting information about others that can be used against the people about whom data has been gathered. From the beginning of civilization, those who had information often had an advantage over those who did not have information. Wars have been won because spies are able to obtain information about the enemy that can be used to gain a strategic advantage in the battlefield. Going beyond the battlefield, knowing the secrets of other people could offer power over others, because the critical information can be used at the appropriate time.

Collecting information about others, however, is a tedious process. Spies usually want to collect the information in a clandestine manner, because the usefulness of spying is lost when the victim becomes aware of the spying. Those who want to collect information need to do so in a secretive way, which is an especially difficult task if sensitive information is kept as data recorded on paper stored in secure locations. The spy will need to get to the location to collect the information, which sometimes makes it impossible to actually collect all the information without disclosing that the secrecy has been compromised. This could make the victim aware of the spying, allowing him or her to deal with the fact that some information has been leaked. The analog storing of information was also simpler, because special precautions could be taken to guard the information well. This helped ensure that spies would not be able to gain access to the locations where the information would be stored.

The matter becomes quite difficult, however, with digital information. There is no unique location of the digital files where the information is stored. Files could be stored in many different places ranging from the hard drive of a computer to portable memory devices that can hold large amounts of information. When dealing with digital information, the spy does not have to deal with truck-loads of paper but only with binary data that can be transferred simply by copying the files from one computer to another. Since many computers are connected to different networks, the spy might not even have to be physically close to the computer to steal the information. A skilled digital spy might be able to take advantage of weak points in a computer network to access information. The victim could be completely unaware of intrusions, because the data spy could obtain data without leaving any trace of the entry. The digital data is not only easier to collect, but it is also possible to ana-lyze large amounts of digital data, since computers can be entrusted with that task. Powerful computers can sift through large amounts of digital information to make connections between the data and real-life events.

CONNECTING DIGITAL INFORMATION AND REAL-LIFE INFORMATION

Extracting useful information from large amounts of data hap-pens through the analysis process. Institutions that are interested in obtaining sensitive information look at many different sources of data to understand the real-life implications of the information. For example, military strategists are often interested in learning about the specific plans of enemy troop movements. Different kinds of digital information, like digital photographs from satellite and digital communication among enemy troops, can be analyzed to uncover the real-life plans. The computer can be an important tool in managing the information and presenting it for analysis by experts, who can observe different sets of data and draw conclusions from them. Some of the analysis can be conducted automatically, but it is usually necessary for experts to draw some conclusions themselves. This is why the Central Intelligence Agency (CIA) of the United States has positions like open source officer (OSO): A person in this job who, according to the CIA Web site, would "review and assess foreign open media sources, including Internet sites, newspapers, press agencies, television, radio and specialized publications." This is a person whose principal job is to connect the digital information with real-life events, so that the U.S. government can have a good sense of what foreign governments are thinking or doing.

One of the most important kinds of information that is tracked to learn about real-life plans of the enemy is the digital communication that goes on within its organization. The importance of this type of information has been recognized in most conflicts. As mentioned before in a previous chapter, in World War II the German coding machine called Enigma was a vital tool in helping Nazi Germany deliver secret messages within its military system. When an Enigma machine was finally captured, it allowed Allied forces to monitor secret communication between submarines at sea and the German naval headquarters. The ability to decipher these messages provided critical intelligence that helped the Allies win the war.

In the digital age, communication takes place using modern, everyday media, including the Internet and telephones. The next sections look at the ways in which it is possible to keep track of the data being sent over modern communication channels.

LISTENING TO CONVERSATIONS

Listening in on private conversations is an age-old spying method. Since information exchanged in these conversations can contain significant strategic information, spies have been trained to become accustomed with the different channels used for communication. One of the most popular methods for carrying out private conversations is the telephone, and spying agencies have developed various ways of eavesdropping on these conversations. For example, in 1999, the U.S. government expelled a Russian diplomat from Washington, D.C., because the person had placed a device in a conference room in the U.S. State Department, compromising the information that had been discussed in meetings and conferences held in that particular room. The BBC reported the story, saying, "It is believed the listening device was planted in a conference room at the State Department where high-level talks are held." These traditional processes used microphones and instruments that could be connected to the traditional telephone that allowed the eavesdropper to listen to the conversation.

The process has evolved, as digital tools can capture entire conversations, digitize the material, and then make it available for a large number of analysts. It is no longer necessary to deal with analog recording tools such as tape recorders, since tiny digital instruments can record large amounts of conversation to be analyzed later.

One of the main challenges with recording telephone conversations is deciding which particular conversation to monitor for information. In a country like the United States, nearly everyone has a phone connection, and there are millions of phone conversations going on every day. It would be an overwhelming task to keep track of all the conversations by recording them. On the other hand, because a significant amount of the telephone technology has become digital, an instant record is created of every phone call, which notes the phone number from which the call was made, the number that was called, the time of the call, and the duration of the call. Every telephone consumer gets these details with the monthly bill. Government spy agencies can have access to the millions of records of phone calls that are made, which can then be analyzed using a computer. The analysis can reveal specific patterns of phone calls, which can help agencies determine which phone conversations may warrant careful vigilance—for example, if a pattern is suspicious or of particular interest. This process of filtering out the innocent phone calls has been made possible because telephone companies are able to maintain a digital record of every phone call.

Usually the objective of spying on phone calls is not to obtain a complete record of the exact words spoken in every phone call. The more important issue is to discover who is speaking to whom, because that information can provide indications of where dangerous conversations are going on. This is what the National Security Agency (NSA) does in the United States, where it is allowed to secretly collect the phone records of millions of Americans. According to a 2006 *USA Today* article, "The spy agency is using the data to analyze calling patterns in an effort to detect terrorist activity." Only conversations that appear to be suspicious would actually be recorded for analysis, creating a manageable number of recordings for analysis. A computer can point toward the suspicious conversations by looking for key phone numbers and names in the vast database of all phone call records. Later, a human analyst would need to listen to the conversation to determine if indeed there are some threats in the recorded conversation. Although the computer is usually incapable of analyzing spoken words, it can analyze digital code by keeping track of e-mail exchanges.

TRACKING DIGITAL COMMUNICATION

The most prevalent form of digital communication is the e-mail. It is difficult to exactly estimate the number of e-mails sent each day, but one study in 2008 estimated the number of e-mails sent per day was 210 billion. An e-mail is made up of two main digital parts: One part has information about the destination of the e-mail, while the other part is the content of the e-mail. Usually an e-mail originates from a personal computer that is networked to the Internet. The first part of the e-mail contains instructions for the computer about how to route the e-mail. This routing could involve the content of the e-mail being bounced among numerous computers on the Internet until it reaches the final destination. Most of the routing happens very rapidly, which ensures that the e-mail content reaches its destination in the shortest possible time. Since the digital data travels through many points before reaching its destination, however, it is vulnerable to spying. Spying on e-mail requires peeking into the digital data that makes up the content of the e-mail.

In order to spy on e-mails, it is necessary to develop a system that can unobtrusively retain a copy of the digital data as it passes through a specific computer on its way to the destination. All e-mails have to go through at least one computer other than the one from which it originated. This is the computer that provides an e-mail account to a user. For example, if someone has an e-mail account with a corporation like Yahoo!, then an e-mail has to pass through a computer operated by Yahoo!. It is possible to place a data-capturing tool on the Yahoo! computer. Neither the sender nor the receiver would realize that a copy of the e-mail has been stored for future reference. A company called DS Development advertises exactly such a product called "Silentmail." According to the company's Web site, Silentmail can "silently monitor outlook emails." A company could install such a program to monitor every e-mail that goes through the company e-mail gateway. The main problem with such monitoring is the volume of digital data that is generated by the spying process, because thousands of e-mails could quickly clog up storage systems. The large amount of data can also become quite unmanageable from the analytical point of view, as it is not possible for a human being to sift through thousands of e-mails daily to find any meaningful information. The e-mails capture system has to be supplemented with efficient digital analysis to make sense of the data collected.

The main way of interpreting e-mail data is to look for specific patterns in the data. These patterns can become behavioral indicators; they suggest that people who send e-mails using specific methods or language can indicate how the person behaves in real life. This interpretation requires special computer programs that are able to examine the digital data to make sense of the information. This computing capacity is usually available to governments and other very large institutions. For example, in a 2006 article in *The Christian Science Monitor*, staff writer Mark Clayton wrote about "a little-known system called Analysis, Dissemiation, Visualization, Insight, and Semantic Enhancement (ADVISE). Only a few public documents mention it. ADVISE is a research and development program within the Department of Homeland Security (DHS), part of its three-year-old 'Threat and Vulnerability, Testing and Assessment' portfolio. The TVTA received nearly $50 million in federal funding this year." The main function of the system is "sifting through data to look for patterns," according to Clayton. These expensive systems can be used to monitor e-mails and other digital messages, such as text messages.

From a military and national security standpoint, it is also important to have access to information that relates to actual events that are happening throughout the world. These events could involve clandestine movements of people, reassignment of military battalions, and other such activities. This data has become more accessible to agencies with the advent of satellite-based surveillance systems.

USE OF SATELLITES IN COLLECTING INFORMATION

The analysis of digital records of phone calls and the scrutiny of e-mail data offer a wealth of information about suspicious activities, but a good amount of strategic information also comes from observation of enemy behavior. This kind of information might relate to ways that certain countries are preparing for conflict—for example, by lining up troops in specific ways. This information also deals with changes happening in distant places that may serve as visible evidence of hostile activities. Since it might be impossible to put a spy in the enemy territory, many nations collect information about enemy behavior by observing enemy territory from space using spy satellites that generate digital data.

Satellites that orbit the Earth can use extremely powerful cameras to take close-up pictures of the ground below. Satellites placed strategically in space can keep an eye on every part of the globe at all times. The images that are produced by the satellites are transmitted back to Earth as digital images, connecting satellite technology with digital technology. The satellites serve as critical tools that are constantly recording digital images.

The images that are sent by the satellites can be manipulated with the use of digital image adjustment tools. The digital images can be analyzed and edited to separate relevant information from useless information. Some of the image manipulation tools could also be used to magnify specific parts of an image to get a closer look at details. Numerous images can be digitally connected to

The thousands of satellites orbiting Earth perform a variety of tasks, including taking photo images for commercial, academic, and government purposes. Analysts working for cell phone companies or even the military can take ordinary satellite images and alter them to enhance the details of any area or region.

create composite images that carry more information than individual images. These manipulations have become possible because of powerful computers that can analyze a large number of digital images. The digitization of satellite images makes it possible to deal

Satellite Surveillance

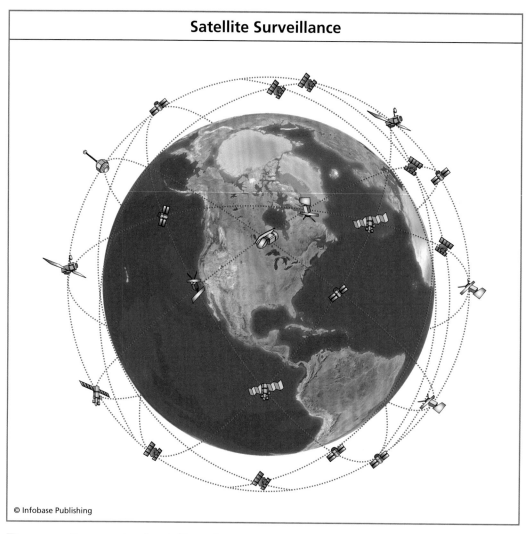

© Infobase Publishing

There are thousands of satellites that create a network of instruments around Earth. These satellites can take powerful pictures and send them instantly to receiving stations. Such information is used by different defense organizations to constantly keep an eye on all parts of the globe.

with the vast amounts of image data that many satellites are constantly producing from space.

The different spying systems generate large amounts of data that is eventually stored in large databases.

ELECTRONIC DATABASES TO KEEP RECORDS

The different processes of data collection eventually result in the production of extremely large sets of information. As discussed, governments and large corporations are able to collect huge amounts of information about people, much of which is retained as digital data. Social Security numbers and other specific identification numbers are central pieces of information, as they are associated with nearly everything the person does. They show up in financial records, educational records, driving records, and many other digital data sets that track a person's life. Each of these records represents a separate set of digital data. The identification number can be used to combine the different digital data sets to create a composite digital database for an individual.

Combined databases can be produced for everyone in a country. This would create extremely large databases that could digitally capture the private information of thousands, and even millions, of people. These databases could then be analyzed to track the behavior and habits of people. The results of such analysis could be used for good and bad purposes. On one hand, knowing details about a specific group of people can allow better service to be provided to that group. For example, if there was a national database of everyone with a particular kind of illness, it would be possible to find these people to deliver specific information and treatment. On the other hand, the information about specific groups of people could be used to treat them as second-class citizens simply because they represent a marginal group. This is what was practiced in Nazi Germany in the 1930s and 1940s when lists of Jewish people were developed for future persecution. In the digital age, massive databases could also be used as tools for surveillance and policing.

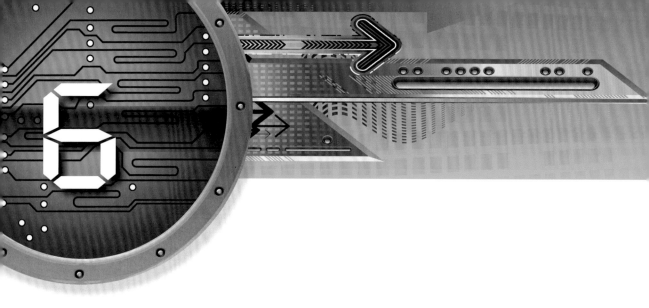

Digital Police

In 2008, the British newspaper *The Telegraph* reported that the British government would soon establish a nationwide police system that would be responsible for tackling digital crime. The government would set up policies that would require greater cooperation between private agencies and law enforcement agencies to ensure that Internet-based criminal activities are reduced. The news report claimed there would be an official minister who would "be directly responsible for co-ordinating policy against cybercrime." The process of controlling illegal Internet activity has been built around national and international police units that are trained to handle digital crime. This new police force possesses special skills that allow its members to monitor the Internet to identify criminal activities. This has led to new "cat-and-mouse" games in which the criminals come up with innovative ways to hide from the digital police. Different laws are quickly being introduced to help control the Internet-based criminal activities throughout the world.

The Internet has been able to dismantle many of the geographic barriers that existed in the world. Before the popularity of the Internet, criminals generally operated within the same general regions and illegal activities were contained within specific geographic areas. In such cases, the criminals were usually charged with breaking the laws of a single nation. A criminal would be put to trial in the country where the law was broken even if a criminal was able to run away to a different place. There are numerous cases in which a criminal would be brought back to the nation where the crime was committed. This is especially true for terrorists who try to set up havens in other nations, as in the case of a terrorist who was hiding in Pakistan in 2006. A *USA Today* story about the return of this person from Pakistan to Britain described the situation, reporting that "[t]he British government has requested the extradition of Rashid Rauf, a Briton arrested in Pakistan earlier this month in connection with the alleged plot to blow up U.S.-bound jetliners." These negotiations help to bring criminals to justice, particularly in a world where it is easy to move from one place to another and hide one's identity using the Internet.

The emergence of the Internet has both altered the geographic boundaries of crime and led to the development of new criminal activities. For example, identity theft as a criminal activity has essentially been reinvented since significant amounts of personal data have been converted to digital files. As discussed previously, the digitization of critical personal information has made stealing another person's identity an extremely common and insidious crime. Before this conversion, identity theft was restricted to thieves using stolen credit cards to purchase goods and services. The thief needed to have physical access to the credit card to be able to use the card. On the other hand, the criminal can now gain access to large amounts of personal information like credit card numbers by skillfully breaking into the computers that store large databases of personal information. The thief does not have to be anywhere near the computer and can gain access to information about multiple people who are widely distributed geographically, and the invasion can be done from thousands of miles away. In these situations, the thief might not even be in the same country as the victim, which makes it particularly difficult to find the thief and bring him or her to justice.

The Internet has also made it much easier to move stolen products across national boundaries. The process of bringing an illegal object from one place to another is called smuggling. Over the decades, various international smuggling networks have operated to traffic in all kinds of illicit products. For example, prohibition laws in the early part of the twentieth century made it illegal to produce or sell alcoholic beverages in the United States. These restrictions led to the development of an efficient smuggling network that illegally brought alcohol into the United States from Canada. This kind of activity can be easy to monitor, as vigilant border police can easily detect suspicious shipments moving across national borders.

Illegal transportation and trading of digital data, however, is far more difficult to control and has led to a new type of international smuggling for the digital age. For example, it is relatively simple to send a digital file from London to Beijing without anyone noticing the transfer, and the high-speed networks allow people to send large files quickly over the Internet. Furthermore, digital files can be easily duplicated and numerous copies can be made of the file. A file containing music can be copied many times, and the music file can be sent out to a large number of people for a nominal cost. This constitutes a digital copyright violation, as material protected by digital copyright laws becomes available at little or no cost. Companies and businesses that were relying on the profits from selling albums and compact discs (CDs) can lose an incredible amount of money as unscrupulous businesses rapidly make thousands of copies of a file and distribute them globally for no cost.

The Internet has made it possible to maintain illicit businesses by providing services and goods that could be banned in one country but legal in another. This is often the case with the trading of pornography, because countries throughout the world have different standards and laws that ban, restrict, or allow this kind of material. To take advantage of such differences, Internet traders could set up

The increase in online shopping sales has been accompanied by a surge in illegal online activity. While most people enjoy the ease and convenience of purchasing items on the Internet, many fail to realize the dangers of sending the details of their private information over the Web.

their computers in the country where it is legal to sell the material and then advertise the product across the world, allowing any user with Internet access to buy the digital product. This criminal activity can also make a criminal of the person who purchases the illegal product, as many of the laws related to pornography on the Internet criminalize both the seller and the buyer of offensive material. For example, the law in the United States says that anyone who knowingly receives pornographic material involving minors is subject to prosecution. In such cases, the seller might be immune to the laws of a country, but the buyer could be prosecuted for buying the product.

As pointed out earlier in the book, the Internet has also made it possible to deceive people in many new ways. Trust on the Internet is often based on how well a person or an institution can present itself on the Internet. A well-designed Web site could generate trust among the users, and the trust can be used to elicit sensitive information about those who visit the Web site. The information that is disclosed at a Web site can then be abused by the criminals who might operate from thousands of miles away. There may be little a person can do once he or she falls prey to one of the large number of deceptions that are on the Internet.

The Internet has also allowed criminals to work together. Criminals have been able to use the communication capabilities of the Internet to stay connected. It is simple to use the Internet for clandestine communication since there are no physical locations associated with an e-mail address. A person could use the same e-mail address from anywhere in the world, or one person could maintain numerous e-mail addresses for different purposes. It could take a long time for law enforcement personnel to track down the different ways in which e-mail has been used to plan and execute criminal activities.

The Internet provides a set of new tools by which the digital component of everyday life can be used for criminal activities. The next sections look at the way in which law enforcement has responded to these new brands of crime.

NATIONAL AND INTERNATIONAL POLICE

Most nations have internal police forces that are responsible for maintaining law and order within the national boundaries. Police from one country are usually not allowed to operate in other countries. There can be cooperation between the police forces, but countries tend to protect their autonomy with respect to their own police forces. Most countries also have police forces for specific parts of the country. For example, in the United States, the police are categorized into city police, county police, state police, and federal police, all of which have different levels of authority. They are expected to work together but are discouraged from interfering with one another's operations.

There is also some degree of competition between the different police forces. The municipal police are responsible for enforcement within the city limits, so the city police might be unwilling to allow the county police to interfere with police work within the city limits. The matter gets far more complicated when different countries are involved, and police in one country might not want interference from the police of another country when trying to solve a crime. A case in point involves British police helping to solve the mystery surrounding the 2008 assassination of the former prime minister of Pakistan. Although the help was eventually accepted, CNN.com reported that "Pakistan's decision to accept Britain's help in the investigation is a dramatic turnaround from the government's position." Initially, the government was reluctant to bring in an outside agency to help with solving an internal mystery.

There is also a general lack of standardized operating procedures for cooperation between police from different countries because of the ways in which police of different countries work within their jurisdictions. For example, different countries have specific ways in which the police are trained, just as there are differences in the limits of what the police force can do. Some countries allow the police to carry handguns, whereas police in other countries, such as Britain, generally do not carry any firearms. There are cultural differences among the police-citizen relationships in different countries as well. For example, in Eastern Europe it is not unusual to be able to bribe a police officer and get away with a traffic offense. As a 2007 news story in the *New York Times* reported, "The corruption also emboldens people to drive recklessly because they know they can skirt penalties by slipping money to an officer. (The typical bribe is $5 to $20.)" While this behavior does not relate directly to cybercrime, it does point toward the way in which police operate in different countries. Such differences pose a challenge when police forces have to deal with criminal activities that span national boundaries.

While the police forces from different nations might find it difficult to work together, criminals are able to use the Internet to run international criminal operations. For example, the illegal use of digital files is not contained within traditional geographic boundaries. This makes it important that policing of illegal Internet activities involves the cooperation of police from many geographic areas. The best mechanism for this cooperation is offered by the Interpol, which is an organization that facilitates "cross-border police co-operation, and supports and assists all organizations, authorities and services whose mission is to prevent or combat international crime."

Interpol was established in 1923 to fight organized crime syndicates that were involved in international criminal activities. The importance of the Interpol has grown as the incidence of international crime has increased. As a result, one of the core functions of Interpol is the maintenance of large digital databases containing information about known international criminals that is accessible to all the members of Interpol. Interpol helps in the sharing of information but is limited in its enforcement functions, so some feel that there needs to be an organization that is specifically charged with controlling international digital crime. For example, the head of an antivirus research laboratory, Eugene Kaspersky, said in 2006 that he would like to see an Internet Interpol that would be able to react quickly to criminal activities that happen on the Internet. This would be an organization that is designed to specifically deal with crime that involves the use of digital resources. Members of this crime-fighting force would need to have special skills that make them ready to work against the criminals who operate within the digital realm.

NEW SKILLS FOR A NEW POLICE

Digital crime often involves rapid transfer of digital information that can travel thousands of miles in an instant. The person involved in digital crime relies on the speed of computing, specific programs that help to hide the identity of the criminal, and the protection afforded by the differences in national laws. The police force fighting the digital criminal has to be responsive to all the different ways in which the digital criminal tries to outwit the law. It needs to become a new kind of force, one that is very aware of the digital technologies being used by criminals, and the police will have to be as competent with the new technologies as the digital criminal—if

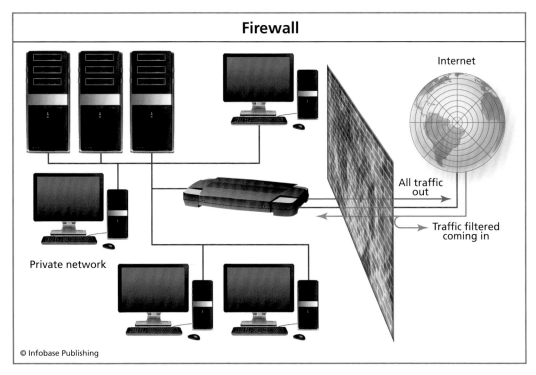

Firewall

Internet

All traffic out

Traffic filtered coming in

Private network

© Infobase Publishing

As in the case of real-life firewalls, the digital firewall acts as a barrier between the Internet and the internal network of a home or institution. The firewall ensures that harmful files cannot penetrate the internal network and that sensitive information is not accidentally shared with the globally available Internet.

not better. For example, if a digital criminal attempts to hide digital evidence, the police must have the capability to detect and retrieve it. The new police also must be able to work across national borders, because a digital file that can be used as evidence of criminal activity might have to be retrieved from a distant place, and the police responsible for controlling digital crime must have the ability to access files independent of where the files are located.

There is increasing awareness among some law enforcement agencies that there need to be new levels of cooperation among different police forces. A news report in the *Wall Street Journal* reported in 2006 that the FBI had increased the number of foreign agents to about 150 people who are assigned to 56 offices throughout the world. These agents work with the local governments to find the criminals who are working across borders. The same news story also reported on the creation of the "Cyber Action Teams, or CATs—a group of about 25 people that includes agents, computer forensic experts and specialists in computer code." This is the new type of police who would potentially be able to deal with the increasing incidence of digital crime. The new police will have to learn the latest digital skills and remain up to date with the technology used by the digital criminal. There also needs to be a better understanding of the ways and means of digital crimes, as the goal of the crime is often to interfere with information infrastructures rather than to directly hurt people. People usually are not killed by digital criminals, so the traditional police mind-set of protecting people and property has to be supplemented by the goal of protecting digital data.

The process of protecting digital data has also led to the reconsideration of the value of data. New international laws are being developed to help protect digital information.

LAWS TO CURB DIGITAL CRIME

Some of the laws created to combat digital crime are meant to protect digital information from misuse. Under these laws, two main kinds of digital information are protected from criminal activity. One is information that requires significant resources to produce; for example, a movie studio can spend billions of dollars to make a movie that is distributed as digital information on digital video discs (DVDs). Moviemakers hope to sell DVDs to recover part of the cost of producing the movie and to make a profit. If the digital product is smuggled out and then sold illegally, the original set of authors cannot make the money they need to continue to operate in the creative industry. Therefore, there are laws that aim to protect the rights of the authors of digital products. These laws have adapted traditional copyright laws, which help ensure that intellectual property is not stolen.

The second type of protected digital information is the identifying data about people, contained in vast databases. As discussed earlier, these databases could carry a digital image of a person, which criminals could steal and misuse. There are laws related to identity theft that discourage such criminal activities and protect the information as well as the person whose information might be stolen. These laws are meant to prosecute the people who obtain information about others and then use that information for personal gain. Some countries value the privacy of the information more than other countries, and in these countries—including America—there are more stringent laws for the protection of private information. For example, the Health Insurance Portability and Accountability Act (HIPAA) of 1996 outlines strict regulations about who may have access to the health information of Americans. In some cases, the HIPAA regulations would not allow even close relatives of a patient to gain access to health information unless the patient explicitly permits it. These and other laws that spell out what personal information is meant to remain private have become extremely important in the digital age, because so much personal information is digital and easily accessible.

New laws also have been established to protect against the misuse of the communication networks that have emerged in the digital age. Tools like file-sharing programs allow for trading of digital files that might be difficult to exchange in any other format. For example, there is a documented growth in the trading of pornography with the expansion of the Internet, which has made it simpler for individuals to view global pornographic material on the Web. One 2006 estimate suggested that there were 4.2 million pornographic Web sites available on the Internet. Part of the reason for this is because it is relatively easy to send pornographic images, like most other images, as digital files. As discussed earlier, there are laws that are meant to curb the production, distribution, and use of such images. These laws are also meant to protect the people who might have been abused in the process of creating specific images.

The key purpose of the laws that have emerged with the growth of the Internet is to protect information. A secondary purpose is to protect people who could be involved with the information. Law enforcement agencies must develop specific strategies to help uphold these laws.

ENFORCING THE NEW LAWS

Establishing laws is the first step toward tackling digital crimes, but trained police forces must then enforce the laws that have been established. As discussed earlier in the section on police forces, there are some specific challenges associated with the enforcement process. In addition to the problems with police cooperation, the differences between national laws also poses a challenge. Even if laws and policing can be worked out, other challenges remain.

Law enforcement agencies need to become aware of an incident of digital crime in a timely fashion in order to enforce the laws. Often, digital crime can go undetected for a long time. For example, a person might be the victim of identity theft without knowing it. By the time the crime is reported, the criminal could have disappeared out of reach of law enforcement. Proper enforcement of digital crime requires cooperation from the victims, because law enforcement agencies need to have information about a crime as soon as possible in order to apprehend the criminal.

Popular, if sometimes inadvertent, support for certain criminal activities that deal with digital data poses another challenge. Enforcement of laws becomes difficult when the general population is unwilling to cooperate. This is especially true in cases of illegal duplication and distribution of digital information. It is difficult to enforce copyright laws as long as there is implicit support for the production of illegal copies of digital products among buyers. It is the existence of the market for such products that leads to the growth of the illegitimate industry. Enforcement becomes particularly complicated when some of the agents might themselves be associated with the process of stealing digital information. In places such as China and Russia, for example, it might be impossible to enforce laws against the sellers of duplicated digital goods, because the entire industry could be covertly supported by local governments. In some cases the government might claim to be opposed to piracy, but in reality not much is done to stop the illegal activity. In 2004, *Washington Post* writer Peter S. Goodman commented on the problem of piracy in China, noting "that the government is more interested in managing the politics of the problem than curbing the reality."

The problem of enforcement is complicated because many different countries need to be involved in the enforcement process, which leads to differences with the interpretation of laws related to digital crime. Since a good amount of digital crime can cross numerous borders, it is sometimes necessary to apply specific local laws depending on the nature of the crime, even if the criminals might be from a different nation. As a *Wall Street Journal* news story in 2005 reported, "Two Americans working in China, Randolph H. Guthrie III and Abram C. Thrush, received prison sentences in Shanghai for illegally selling $840,000 worth of pirated DVD's and for stashing more than 210,000 of the knock-offs in three warehouses. American and Chinese law enforcement authorities said the pair sold the DVD's on eBay and through a Russian Web site to buyers in almost two dozen countries, including the United States." This shows how many different countries could get involved in the process of enforcement, which makes it a particularly difficult task.

A digital criminal can also elude the law simply by becoming an essentially nationless person, one who operates with a mobile computer and moves around frequently from one place to another. Enforcement of the laws related to digital crime will have to constantly stay current with the changes in technology that make it easier for the digital criminal to fool the enforcement agents.

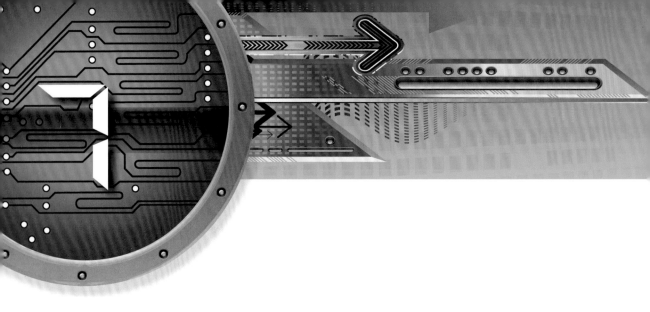

In the Future

This volume has examined some of the key components of digital crime. Unfortunate as it may be, behavior with the intent to do harm has been a long-standing human tendency. All societies have their share of people who are intent on doing harm to others for many different reasons, often relating to personal gain. New digital technologies have offered new opportunities for these unethical—perhaps even evil—people to do their deeds. Digital crime represents a growing concern, and the emergence of crimes using digital technologies has led to the necessary development of new ways of fighting this crime. As discussed here, digital crime does not necessarily cause physical harm the way violent crime does, but criminals operating in the digital realm can cause significant damage to individuals and institutions by interfering with the digital data that represent actual people and entities. The way these virtual crimes cause real-life consequences is the main concern. This chapter examines some of those threats and discusses the steps that could be taken to minimize the threats.

One of the principal future problems is the way in which a terrorist organization could use the information available from the Internet and other digital sources to plan and coordinate real-life attacks. Terrorist organizations like al Qaeda have already been using digital technology for this purpose. A 2004 news story by the BBC described the arrest of a person in Pakistan whose computer contained "an e-mail trail leading directly to a Tanzanian wanted for the 1998 US embassy bombings in East Africa." The popularity of, and easy global access to, the Internet allows cyberterrorists to hide from sight while conducting their malicious business. Police hunting for terrorists in India have found that cyber cafés are used by known terrorists to keep in touch with their leaders in different countries. For example, in 2006, the Indian newspaper *The Hindu* reported that, "After landing in Hyderabad, terrorists have been using cyber cafes as a 'safe place' for easy communication with their associates in Pakistan." The anonymity offered by these cyber cafés offers a sense of security to the terrorists, but some local governments in India have implemented regulations that will curb the relative freedom that was enjoyed by the users of these cafés. Other countries have also created new laws or policies that require Internet café users to sign in with an official picture ID.

In the future, there will also have to be creative use of legislation and enforcement to curb problems while ensuring that the legal, acceptable use of the Internet is not restricted. These laws would have to deal with offensive material on Web sites, the increasing use of spam, and the threat from malicious programs that could invade a computer. For example, starting in 2007, the South Korean government required that certain words be banned from use with search engines like Google. If a person in South Korea wanted to find more information about any of those words, the user must first verify that he or she is over 19 years old. Reporting on this event, Martyn Williams of *IDG News Service* wrote, "Users will be asked to verify their age when searching for any of about 700 words in Korean judged to be adult." Such decisions can quickly become cumbersome, and legitimate users searching for bona fide information could be restricted because some Web users choose to place offensive material on the Internet. These users are also untouchable to law enforcement because they enjoy the protection of the laws of the nation from which they operate.

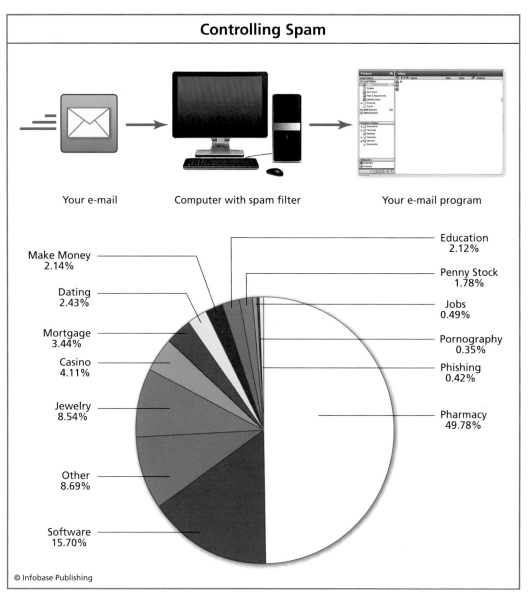

Controlling Spam

Your e-mail

Computer with spam filter

Your e-mail program

- Make Money 2.14%
- Dating 2.43%
- Mortgage 3.44%
- Casino 4.11%
- Jewelry 8.54%
- Other 8.69%
- Software 15.70%
- Education 2.12%
- Penny Stock 1.78%
- Jobs 0.49%
- Pornography 0.35%
- Phishing 0.42%
- Pharmacy 49.78%

© Infobase Publishing

Just like viruses, many undesired e-mails or spam also have specific characteristics, and there are computer programs that scan all e-mail messages and separate out those messages that could be spam. These messages are stored in a special mailbox without crowding the "inbox" of the user.

It will be a challenge to successfully enforce the new laws that would be coming into place to restrict the use of digital tools for illegal purposes. The law enforcement agencies would have to find people who are sufficiently skilled with computer use to detect a cyberattack, stop the attack, and eventually find the attacker. There is increasing recognition of the need for appropriate training of police officers to deal with cybercrime, as demonstrated by the 2007 meeting for law enforcement personnel in the state of Massachusetts. A press release from the Office of the Attorney General of the State of Massachusetts reported that meeting attendees discussed many ideas, including "trends in Internet crimes and investigations, as well as methods used to investigate websites, domain names, IP addresses, email messages, and chat and instant messages." This is the direction that other law enforcement agencies will have to take in order to be able to stay current with the spread of digital crime.

The way in which digital crime spreads in the future will also depend on the way in which people actually use and protect their own computers. The average user will have to become much more proficient with security systems and install necessary safeguards. This is particularly important since most computers are now connected to the Internet. A computer infected with a bad program could easily become the source of viral infection for thousands of other computers, and it is up to the individual computer user to ensure that a personal computer is adequately protected. As Ira Winkler, a specialist in Internet security, stated in a 2008 article in the Web magazine *Internet Evolution,* "The lack of these countermeasures allow[s] computers to be taken over by a malicious party and then used maliciously to either attack other computers, spew out spams, or distribute malware." Adequate protection to counter the effects of harmful programs could go a long way in ensuring that entire computer systems remain unharmed.

The future of digital technology holds a lot of promise, as people continue to find inventive ways to use the latest technologies to enhance the quality of life. It's important to remember, however, that these enhancements come with the responsibility of protection from illegal use. Together we can help ensure that the malicious intent of a few does not jeopardize the benefit that digital technologies provide to all.

Chronology

3100 B.C.	Numbers with 10 base used in Egypt.
A.D. **628**	Indian mathematician Brahmagupta suggests that zero was a real number and offers rules for its use.
1040	Printing press developed in China by the Chinese inventor Bi Sheng, who carved Chinese characters with wood.
1200	The abacus is used to do mathematical calculations in China.
1439	Johannes Gutenberg develops the printing press in Europe.
1666	The idea of the binary number system using zero and one is introduced.
1822	Charles Babbage designs the first mechanical computer, using the idea of binary numbers.
1876	Alexander Graham Bell patents the first telephone.
1904	John Fleming makes the vacuum tube that can be used as an electronic switch.
1923	Interpol established as an international police force to fight international crime.
1927	*The Jazz Singer* is released as the first movie to use sound.
1947	John Bardeen builds the transistor that replaces the vacuum tube.

1948	Howard Aiken develops an electronic computer with 5,000 vacuum tubes.
	Patent issued for Cathode Ray Tube Amusement Device, starting the era of digital games.
1953	IBM introduces the model 604 computer with transistors.
1956	IBM introduces the magnetic hard drive as a storage medium.
1957	IBM introduces the model 608 computer for the commercial market.
1964	John Kemeny and Thomas Kurtz develop the BASIC computer program language.
1967	The analog sound generator Moog synthesizer is adopted by rock band the Monkees.
1969	DARPA funds the development of an international network of computers.
	The lunar module lands on the moon, using a computer smaller in capacity than a personal computer of 2009.
1970	Digital Electronics Corporation introduces the personal dot matrix printer.
1975	Industrial Lights & Magic established by George Lucas to use computer graphics in making movies.
	Byte magazine is launched as the first magazine dealing with digital technology.
	The PLATO networked education system serves 146 locations in Illinois.
1977	Apple Corporation introduces the Apple II computer.
1978	Roy Trubshaw, a student at Essex University in the United Kingdom, starts working on a multiuser adventure game called *MUD* (*Multiuser Dungeon*).

1980   Polydor Company of Hanover, Germany, produces the commercially available compact disc.

Pac-Man game released in Japan.

1981   Microsoft develops the DOS computer program as the operating system for computers.

IBM introduces the first personal computer using the MS-DOS operating system.

1982   The Groupe Spécial Mobile (GSM) cell phone technology is developed by the Conference of European Posts and Telecommunications (CEPT).

The compact disc is introduced in the United States.

1985   Intel introduces the 80386 microprocessor, with 275,000 transistors built into the chip.

The computer program WELL is set up to allow a community of people to exchange computer files with one another.

The C++ computer language is released commercially.

1986   The Farooq Alvi brothers, operating out of Lahore, Pakistan, release the first computer virus called "The Brain."

1987   German scientist Dieter Seitzer develops the mp3 format for digitizing sound.

1989   The European Center for Particle Research (CERN) in Switzerland invents the World Wide Web.

SimCity developed as an alternative to shoot-up digital games.

Nintendo introduces the Game Boy in the United States.

1990   Commercially available digital still camera sold by Logitech.

Code Division Multiple Access (CDMA) cell phone technology is developed by Qualcomm.

1992 First Short Message Service (SMS) message sent from a cell phone.

1993 Intel introduces the Pentium microprocessor, with 3.1 million transistors built into the chip.

Researchers at the University of Illinois at Urbana-Champaign introduce Mosaic as a tool to browse data on the Web.

1995 *Toy Story* is produced by using only computer-generated images to create a complete movie.

Presidential Savings Bank is the first bank to provide the option of doing financial transactions on the computer.

Pierre Omidyar, a French-born Iranian computer scientist, establishes the prototype for the online auction Web site eBay.

1996 Health Insurance Portability and Accountability Act (HIPAA) is introduced, placing strict regulations about who may have access to the health information of Americans.

Palm introduces the personal digital assistant (PDA).

Travelocity.com launches an online system for selling airline tickets.

1997 The digital video disc (DVD) is introduced in the United States.

Movies begin to be released on DVDs.

TiVo is introduced to digitally capture television shows.

Instant Messaging (IM) technology is introduced by companies like America Online (AOL).

"Deep Blue" computer beats Garry Kasparov at chess.

1998	The United States adopts the Digital Millennium Copyright Act (DMCA), which offers extensive legal protection to the creators and distributors of digital products.
	Printed version of *Byte* is discontinued after 23 years in publication, having been the first magazine to deal with digital technologies.
	New Media & Society is launched by Sage Publications to examine the role of digital technologies in society.
	The Motion Picture Experts Group standardizes the MP4 format for capturing and storing digital video.
	Google begins with a $100,000 investment as a company operating from a garage.
2000	Nearly 5,000 satellites are in space.
	Trek Technology and IBM introduce the flash memory as a storage medium.
	Google becomes the most popular Internet search tool.
2001	Apple introduces the iPod.
	Wikipedia is launched as a freely editable online encyclopedia.
2003	Linden Research Laboratories introduces Second Life as a multiuser social game.
	United Nations Educational, Scientific and Cultural Organization (UNESCO) begins a special award on digital art through their "DigiArts" mission.
	MySpace is introduced as a social networking Web site.
2004	Two-thirds of Americans claim to use instant messaging on a regular basis.
	Liberated Syndication offers the first podcast hosting service for a $5 monthly fee.

Revenue from the sale of digital games doubles from the 1994 sales level.

The Food and Drug Administration (FDA) approves the use of an embedded microprocessor in the human body for medical purposes.

2005 Steve Chen, Chad Hurley, and Jawed Karim introduce YouTube.

In one of the largest breaches of the security of personal information, 40 million Visa and MasterCard credit card numbers become available to anyone on the Internet.

Ninety percent of all videos sold in China are illegally produced pirated copies of the original DVD.

Microsoft introduces the Xbox 360 game system.

In the United States, the number of identity thefts exceeds 250,000.

Google introduces Google Maps as a digital mapping tool.

2006 Eleven years after its launch, eBay has 200 million registered users worldwide.

Sony introduces the PlayStation3 game system.

Nintendo introduces the Wii game system.

Sun Microsystems releases Java as a computer program that anyone can freely use.

Facebook becomes available to anyone in the world.

In Britain, the number of surveillance cameras reaches 4.2 million, 1 for every 14 people.

On average, the number of spam e-mails sent per day reaches 12.4 billion.

2007 In a single month, more than 24 million users visit the YouTube Web site.

American consumers spend about $30 billion shopping on the Internet during the Christmas shopping season.

Sales of the LCD screen surpass sales of the CRT screen worldwide.

Apple introduces the iPhone.

James Cameron and Vince Pace develop the 3-D Fusion Camera System to shoot feature films in stereo-scopic 3-D. It is used to shoot several films, including *Aliens of the Deep*, *The Adventures of Sharkboy and Lava-girl*, and *Ghosts of the Abyss*.

2008   The number of airline tickets sold on the Internet exceeds the number sold through travel agents and other offline systems.

2009   All television stations in the United States begin broad-casting digital signals.

2010   James Cameron's film *Avatar*, which is made almost entirely of computer-generated animation using the 3-D Fusion Camera System, breaks the record for highest-grossing film of all time. It is also the first movie ever to earn more than $2 billion worldwide.

Glossary

America Online (AOL)   A private company providing Internet access for a fee.

analog   A signal that delivers data continuously in time and amplitude; can be converted into a digital signal.

Apple Corporation   A private company manufacturing digital goods.

archive   A collection of historical records of information.

Atari   A private company manufacturing digital game products.

binary system   A system that represents numeric values using only two digits, usually zero and one.

Bose Corporation   A private company manufacturing audio systems like speakers.

British Broadcasting Corporation (BBC)   The state-owned radio and television broadcasting organization in Great Britain.

broadband   A method of sending digital information that allows a large amount of information to be sent in a short time.

buffer   A temporary space where digital information can be stored for a short period while the computer processes the information.

C++ language   A widely used computer programming language used in a large range of applications.

Center for Disease Control (CDC)   An American government agency that is concerned with the health and safety of people.

chat room   A type of computer program available on the Internet that allows several people to communicate with one another in real time.

compact disc (CD)   A storage medium for music or computer data.

computation   A specific mathematical operation, such as an addition or subtraction, performed by a digital tool like a cell phone.

computer code   A series of letters and numbers that makes up the instructions given to a computer.

computer monitor   A device that acts as the interface between the user and the computer, showing the texts and images produced by the computer.

computer program   A series of commands given to a computer, instructing the computer to perform a series of tasks.

data storage system   A way to permanently save large amounts of digital information.

digital   A quantity, measurement, or signal represented by a series of discrete numbers; an analog signal can be converted into a digital one by sampling its value at periodic intervals.

digitize   The process of converting a continuous quantity, having a numerical value at each instant, to a quantity represented by discrete numbers.

download   A process of moving digital information from a centralized repository of data to a personal digital device like a personal computer.

electron   An atomic particle having a negative charge; currents flowing in many conductors, such as metals, consist primarily of electrons in motion.

electronic bulletin board   A computer program that allows group members to send information to a centralized computer so that all group members can access the information.

Entertainment Software Rating Board (ESRB)   A self-regulatory American organization that calibrates entertainment products like computer games and other digital entertainment products based on suitability for different age groups.

fiber-optic line   A cable that uses pulsating light to transmit digital information.

forum   A computer program that allows a group of people to exchange digital information by placing the information on a centralized computer accessible to all group members.

Game Boy   The trademark of a handheld digital device used for playing digital games.

handheld controller   A portable device, like a small remote control, that is used to control the operations of a digital device.

handheld game machine   A portable digital device that is used to play digital games.

hard drive   A device that is used in digital machines to store information.

high-speed connection   Same as BROADBAND, a method of sending digital information that allows a large amount of information to be sent in a short time.

intellectual property   A legal right of ownership over the creations of the mind, such as music, art, literature, and scientific ideas.

interactive   Describing a process in which every step of the process is dependent on the previous step, as in the case of a conversation in which each message is based on what was just said.

International Business Machine (IBM)   A multinational company that pioneered the manufacture of a computer for personal use.

Internet   The connection of numerous computers where each computer can interact with any other computer on the network.

Java   A special type of computer program that has become very popular for use with Web sites, because the programs can be interpreted by any kind of computer.

keyboard   A device that has a button for every letter of an alphabet and is used by computer users to interact with computers.

local area network (LAN)   A connection between computers that are spatially close to each other, as in the case of a set of computers in a private home.

Magnavox   An American company specializing in the manufacture of home electronic products like televisions, radios, and DVD players.

memory   A component in a digital device that is used to store information, both for long periods of time and short periods of time while the device does computations.

microprocessor   A component in a digital device that contains microscopic electronic switches that are etched onto a tiny piece of silicon, making up the most important part of all digital devices.

Microsoft   An American company that produces the Windows operating systems used in computers worldwide.

mouse   A device used with a computer to simulate the movement of a pointer on the computer screen by moving the physical pointing device on a flat surface.

nationality   The identity of a person based on a person's citizenship documents, such as passports.

networked   A process that connects different digital devices with each other.

networked environment   A working condition where many different digital devices are connected to one another.

Nintendo   A Japanese company that manufactures and sells hand-held computer games, devices, and digital game systems.

Nintendo DS   A more advanced version of GAME BOY.

nodal computer   A machine that makes up the center of a network of computers.

personal computer (PC)   A machine that can be used by a single individual as a personal computer to perform many different digital tasks.

personal digital assistant (PDA) A handheld digital device that keeps a record of contacts, appointments, tasks, and other personal information.

platform The fundamental computer program, like WINDOWS, that provides the support for a large range of computer programs.

PlayStation A personal digital gaming device created by Sony that has the characteristics of a personal computer and also contains a built-in high-definition DVD player.

process A specific set of tasks that a digital device performs to provide a specific function like large statistical calculations.

refresh The way in which the image on a COMPUTER MONITOR is periodically updated to reflect changes in information sent to the computer.

shooting games A category of digital games that uses a replica of a gun or cannon to shoot at objects on the screen.

Sony A Japanese company specializing in the manufacture of home electronic products such as computers, televisions, radios, and DVD players.

statistics A special branch of mathematics focusing on creating estimates and trends by looking at a large amount of data about a specific phenomenon.

text-based message A form of communication that uses only letters of the alphabet.

virtual Any system or phenomenon that only exists as a digital file without any tangible component.

web-based magazine A category of publications that does not have a paper version but exists only on the Internet.

Web The short and colloquial term for the World Wide Web computer program that uses a universal computer language to exchange different kinds of digital information among computers connected to the Internet.

Wii A personal digital gaming created by Nintendo that uses wireless, motion-controlled remotes.

Xbox A personal digital gaming device created by Microsoft that has the characteristics of a personal computer and also contains a built-in high-definition DVD player.

Bibliography

Biever, C. "Modern romance." *New Scientist*, 190 (2549) April 29, 2006.

Bryan-Low, C. "Criminal Network: To Catch Crooks In Cyberspace, FBI Goes Global"; "Agency Works With Police In Foreign Countries To Track Down Hackers." *Wall Street Journal*, A1. November 21, 2006.

Clayton, M. "US plans massive data sweep." *The Christian Science Monitor*. February 9, 2006. Available online. URL: http://www.csmonitor.com/2006/0209/p01s02-uspo.html.

Filiol, E. *Computer Viruses: from theory to applications*. France: Springer Verlag, 2005.

Goodman, P. S. "Pirated Goods Swamp China." *The Washington Post*. September 7, 2004. Available online. URL: http://www.washington post.com/wp-dyn/articles/A535-2004Sep6.html.

Green, J. "The myth of cyber terrorism: There are many ways terrorists can kill you—computers aren't one of them." *Washington Monthly*. November 2002. Available online. URL: http://findarticles.com/p/articles/mi_m1316/is_11_34/ai_94775087/.

Haschak, G. "Another Carpentersville resident's identity stolen—this one 7 years old." *The Daily Herald*. February 23, 2008. Available online. URL: http://www.dailyherald.com/story/?id=140579.

Kahney, L. "Fake CNN Website Taken Offline." *Wired*. February 3, 2003. Available online. URL: http://www.wired.com/culture/lifestyle/news/2003/02/57506.

Krim, J., and M. Barbaro. "40 Million Credit Card Numbers Hacked." *The Washington Post*. June 18, 2005. Available online. URL: http://www.washingtonpost.com/wp-dyn/content/article/2005/06/17/AR2005061701031.html.

Lemos, R. "Defending Your Identity"; "Hardly a week goes by without companies and universities losing digital identities. What can be done?" *PC Magazine,* 25 (12), 1 June 21, 2006.

Maney, K. and M. Kessler. "AOL's tech chief quits after breach of privacy." *USA Today.* August 21, 2006. Available online. URL: http://www.usatoday.com/tech/news/internetprivacy/2006-08-21-aol-privacy-departures_x.htm

Mitra, A. "Trust, authenticity, and discursive power in cyberspace." *Communications of the ACM,* 45 (3), p. 27. 2002.

Moore, S. "Digital Deceptions." *Byte,* 17 (5), p. 372. 1992.

Neely, K. "Notes From the Virus Underground." *Rolling Stone.* September 1999.

Scheeres, J. "Games Elevate Hate to Next Level." *Wired.* February 20, 2002. Available online. URL: http://www.wired.com/culture/lifestyle/news/2002/02/50523.

Thorsberg, F. "The World's Worst Viruses." *PC World.* Aug. 23, 2002. Available online. URL: http://www.pcworld.com/article/103992/the_worlds_worst_viruses.html.

Williams, M. "Google Korea Restricts Search." *PC World.* May 17, 2007. Available online. URL: http://www.pcworld.com/article/131948/google_korea_restricts_search.html.

Winkler, I. "The Most Despicable Users of the Internet." *Internet Evolution.* March 31, 2001. Available online. URL: http://www.internetevolution.com/author.asp?section_id=515&doc_id=149518.

Wolak, J., K. Mitchell, and D. Finkelhor. "Escaping or Connecting? Characteristics of Youth Who Form Close Online Relationships." *Journal of Adolescence* 26 (1), p. 105–19. 2003.

Young, S., and D. Aitel. *The Hacker's Handbook: The Strategy Behind Breaking into and Defending Networks.* Boca Raton: Auerbach Publishers, 2005.

Further Resources

Books

Berners-Lee, Tim. *Weaving the Web: The Original Design and Ultimate Destiny of the World Wide Web*. New York: HarperCollins, 2000.

Campbell-Kelly, Martin and William Aspray. *Computer: A History of the Information Machine*. New York: Westview Press, 2004.

Gates, Bill. *The Road Ahead*. New York: Penguin Books, 1995.

Gregg, John R. *Ones and Zeros: Understanding Boolean Algebra, Digital Circuits, and the Logic of Sets*. New York: Wiley & Sons–IEEE, 1998.

Hafner, Katie and Matthew Lyon. *Where Wizards Stay Up Late: The Origins of the Internet*. New York: Simon & Schuster, 1996.

Jenkins, Henry. *Convergence Culture: Where Old and New Media Collide*. New York: New York University Press, 2006.

———. *Fans, Bloggers, and Gamers: Media Consumers in a Digital Age*. New York: New York University Press, 2006.

Lessig, Lawrence. *Remix: Making Art and Commerce Thrive in the Hybrid Economy*. New York: Penguin Books, 2008.

Negroponte, Nicholas. *Being Digital*. New York: Knopf, 1995.

Nye, David E. *Technology Matters: Questions to Live With*. Cambridge: Massachusetts Institute of Technology Press, 2006.

Palfrey, John and Urs Gasser. *Born Digital: Understanding the First Generation of Digital Natives*. New York: Basic Books, 2008.

Schneier, Bruce. *Secrets and Lies: Digital Security in a Networked World*. New York: Wiley & Sons, 2000.

White, Ron and Tim Downs. *How Computers Work, 8th ed*. Indianapolis: Que Publishing, 2005.

Web Sites

Centers for Disease Control and Prevention

http://www.cdc.gov

A government-run Web site that has information related to effects of computer use on health.

Central Intelligence Agency

https://www.cia.gov/library/publications/the-world-factbook

Web site of the U.S. Government intelligence agency that provides information about digital crime all over the world. The CIA Factbook is also a good source of information about different places.

Entertainment Software Association (ESA)

http://www.theesa.com

U.S. association exclusively dedicated to serving the business and public affairs needs of companies that publish computer and video games for video game consoles, personal computers, and the Internet.

Exploratorium: The Museum of Science, Art and Human Perception

http://www.exploratorium.edu

An excellent web resource containing much information on the scientific explanations of everyday things.

Geek.com

http://www.geek.com

Resource for news and developments on all aspects of digital technology.

HighDef Forum

http://www.highdefforum.com

This Web-based forum offers information related to the developments in digital and high definition video.

HowStuffWorks, Inc.
http://www.howstuffworks.com
Contains a large number of articles, generally written by knowledgeable authors, explaining the science behind everything from computers to electromagnetism.

Institute of Electrical and Electronics Engineers
http://www.ieee.com
International organization involved in the study of computers.

International Communication Association
http://www.icahdq.org
The association offers Web-based resources to understand how human communication works in general and in the context of digital technologies.

Interpol Cybercrime Page
http://www.interpol.int/public/TechnologyCrime/Default.asp
Contains information on the efforts Interpol, an international police organization, is making to prevent digital crime in different regions.

Library of Congress
http://www.loc.gov/index.html
This excellent Web site is a resource for doing research on many different topics using digital technology.

Motion Picture Association of America
http://www.mpaa.org
This Web site offers information on how the different digital music and video formats have evolved and explores the current issues regarding digital video and music.

Psychology Matters
http://psychologymatters.apa.org
A Web site with information on the psychological aspects of computer use.

Science Daily
http://www.sciencedaily.com
Links to information on the developments in basic science research that have an impact on the development of digital technologies.

Picture Credits

Page

16: © Infobase Publishing

21: © Infobase Publishing

22: © Infobase Publishing

32: © Infobase Publishing

41: © Infobase Publishing

46: © Infobase Publishing

53: © Infobase Publishing

59: © Infobase Publishing

62: Shutterstock

65: © Infobase Publishing

77: Satellite map. Courtesy EAA Airventure.

78: © Infobase Publishing

83: Shutterstock

87: © Infobase Publishing

94: © Infobase Publishing

Index

About the Author

Ananda Mitra, Ph.D. is the chair of the Department of Communication at Wake Forest University. He teaches courses on technology, popular culture, issues related to South Asia, and research methods. He has been a technology commentator for regional, national, and international media, such as *Time* magazine. Mitra has published articles in leading communications journals as well as two books.

WITHDRAWN